Are You Prepared to Walk in Your Calling?

Nancy F. Lowery

Are You Prepared to Walk in Your Calling?

ISBN: 9798853955561

Unless otherwise noted, all Scriptures are taken from the King James Version of the Bible (KJV)

NKJV – NEW KING JAMES VERSION
NIV – NEW INTERNATIONAL VERSION
NLT – NEW LIVING TRASLANTION
TLB – THE LIVING BIBLE

Printed in the United States of America

Foreword

Have you ever engaged in Spiritual Warfare, and it felt like you were the last man standing, and you needed a smidgen of encouragement to keep fighting on? Have you ever asked the question, "Lord, have you really chosen me to be picked on for this particular battle?" "Am I that Chosen Vessel?" Lord, you said, **many** are called, but few are **chosen**, but why ME? When your back seems to be against the wall, and the only way out, is to go through, you ask the question: "God, are you up to something concerning ME?" Nevertheless, not **my** will, but **thy** will be done!

Have you ever cried out to the Lord, "I need a Word from You; A "RHEMA" WORD, RIGHT NOW! Just ONE WORD that can change my life. Has your request ever been: Oh Lord, please hearken unto my cry? Has it ever occurred to you that you are not alone? For **many** are the afflictions of the righteous, but God has and will deliver us out of them **all.** It is because He has given us Spiritual Weapons of Mass Destruction!

As a result of reading the numerous books that Apostle Lowery has penned, I have found myself being processed and transformed daily, into the image and likeness of Christ. I have found Apostle Lowery not only to be an inspiring woman of God, but a wonderful mentor. Over the years, I have witnessed her being a woman with Christ-like character, and she also has a Spirit of Excellence. Anything she embarks upon, whether ministering at conferences, aiding in the community, supporting other ministries, or baking pound cakes, she does it all with a pure heart!

As the Lord continues pouring into her, as she pours out to others, I have nothing but Great Expectations, where God will lead her next. I thank God for her wisdom, spiritual discernment, her personal experiences and the revelation knowledge that God has allowed her to share with others. I wait with Great Expectation as God elevates her higher and where He will venture her next.

For now, I am patiently waiting for the completion of her next book. No doubt it will be spiritual food for our souls!

~ Elder Sharlette Graham
Grace Tabernacle of Prayer, Charlotte, NC

Endorsements

Nancy, you are a beautiful and anointed woman of God. You truly have a calling on your life, and you are armored with the Word of God. I have known you for many years and have seen your walk with the Lord. You've trusted Him in your most vulnerable hours. Even in your darkest hours, you encourage others…you encourage **me**. You always have a positive message, a word from God, to give for any occasion.

You love family, you love friends, and you are a bridge that tries to keep us connected. You have a special calling on your life, and I thank God for you. You are a blessing to me and the family. Continue to trust God, keep writing, and be **all** God calls you to be.

I LOVE YOU.

~ Your Cousin

Minister, Dianna W. Bellamy

My wife Nancy has been writing ever since I've known her. She's always taking notes and documenting everything! Nancy has gone from journaling to writing BOOKS.

This awesome woman has been the love of my life for over 45 years, and I couldn't ask for a better wife. She loves the Lord with all her heart, and she is a devoted mother to our daughter Teyshana.

My wife is intelligent, a great homemaker, an excellent steward over our finances and a very stylish dresser.

I'm very proud of Nancy and I support her 100% as an anointed Preacher and Author.

~ Malcom Angelo Lowery
Nancy's Husband A.K.A. Her Honey Bunny

TRAILBLAZERS & WORLD CHANGERS

Monumental Moments in History (2021-2022)

Bianca Smith: The first black woman to be hired as a Coach in Professional Baseball by the Boston Red Sox.

Raye Montague: This trailblazing Engineer became the first person in history to design a Naval Ship using a computer. She smashed both gender and racial barriers to revolutionize ship design and became the U.S. Navy's first female program manager of ships.

Joseph R. Biden: The 46th President of the United States was the oldest President to take office at the age of 78.

Kamala D. Harris: The 49th Vice President of the United States, who was also the first female, as well as the first woman of color to ever hold this esteemed office.

Douglas Emhoff: The first Second Gentleman of the United States who is married to Kamala Harris.

Amanda Gorman: The youngest Poet Laureate to ever speak at a Presidential Inauguration in 2021. She was also the first Poet Laureate to ever perform at the Super Bowl.

Tampa Bay Buccaneers: The first team to play the Super Bowl in its home stadium in the 55 years the game has been held (Feb. 7, 2021).

Bruce Arians: The oldest coach to win a Super Bowl at age 68, as the Tampa Bay Buccaneers defeated the Kansas City Chiefs, 31-9 (Feb. 7,2021).

Alena Analeigh Wicker: A 12-year-old black prodigy from Ft. Worth, Texas, graduated from High School and was accepted into Medical School at age 13. She aspires to work for NASA one day.

Zaila Avant-Garde: A 14-year-old who was the first black to win the Scripts National Spelling Bee Contest on July 8, 2021. She also holds several Guinness's World Records for being able to dribble multiple basketballs simultaneously.

On January 6, 2021: The United States Capitol Building in Washington, DC was attacked by an angry mob of Trump supporters, following his defeat in the 2020 Presidential election.

Phil Mickelson: Became the oldest major championship winner in PGA history at the age of 50, on May 23, 2021.

Tom Brady: The oldest quarterback at the age of 43 to win seven Super Bowl Championships.

Jennifer King: The NFL's first black female to coach full time for the Washington Commanders (formerly known as the Redskins) in 2021.

Rosalind "Roz" Brewer: The first woman and the first woman of color to lead Walgreen's chain as CEO in 2021.

Kim Janey: The first black and the first female to

become acting mayor of Boston, Massachusetts for eight months in 2021.

Queen Elizabeth II: At the age of 96, celebrated her Platinum Jubilee of 70 years on the Royal throne in June of 2022. She was the oldest reigning British Monarch who passed on September 8,2022.

The Honorable Ketanji Brown Jackson: Was sworn in as the first Black woman of the Supreme Court of the United States on June 30, 2022.

On Monday, August 30, 2021: All U.S. troops were pulled out of Afghanistan, after 20 years, making it the longest war ever in American history.

Nischelle Turner: Became the first black woman to co-host Entertainment Tonight in its 40-year history in March of 2021.

Terence Blanchard: Became the first black composer of the Metropolitan Opera on September 27, 2021.

On March 29, 2022: President Joe Biden signed into law the Emmett Till Anti Lynching Act. This is a United States landmark federal law which makes lynching a federal hate crime.

THE PURPOSE OF THIS BOOK

The purpose of this book is to inform the readers that God has placed a unique **calling** or gift inside of you before you were ever born. When there is a calling on your life, that means there is a specific work for you to do. We're all called to do something in life, and no one person is called to do everything! There are different types of callings, such as preaching, teaching, singing, writing, designing, and so many others.

Responding to God's call on your life is a process which includes time, maturity, prayer, patience, mentoring, dedication, correction, humility, and learning to seek God's face. The Bible states the following in Romans 8:28: "And we know that all things work together for good, to those who love God, to those who are the called according to His purpose".

The callings (gifts, skills, and abilities) on our lives are intended to glorify God and to be a blessing to others. God will help you to become all that He has created and called you to be. Remember this: God doesn't always call the qualified, but He always qualifies the called. You just need to be a willing vessel and trust God's Master Plan for your life.

Table of Contents

Chapter One

You Were Created by God on Purpose

EPHESIANS 2:10 *"For we are His workmanship created in Christ Jesus unto good works, which God hath before ordained that we should walk in them."*

God intentionally created you to do good works. You were created to be used by God, for His glory.

JEREMIAH 29:11 *"For I know the thoughts that I think toward you, saith the Lord, thoughts of peace, and not of evil, to give you an expected end."*

God is up to something concerning YOU.

PHILIPPIANS 1:6 *"Being confident of this very thing, that He that has begun a good work in you, will perform it until the day of Jesus Christ."*

In other words, you can rest assured that

God is behind the scenes helping you to become all that He has created and called you to be. He will never stop working on your behalf, and He will empower, enable, and equip you to perform the plans that He has for your life, until the day that His Son Jesus returns to earth.

God knew what He was doing when He made you. He made you exactly the way that He wanted you to be. You are rare and unique. There is nobody else in the whole wide world exactly like YOU.

God created you for His pleasure.

REVELATION 4:11 *"For you are worthy, O Lord, to receive Glory and Honor and Power. For you have created all things and for your pleasure they are and were created."*

COLOSSIANS 1:16,17 *"For by Him were all things created, that are in heaven, and that are in earth, visible and invisible, whether they be thrones, or dominions, or principalities, or powers;*

all things were created by Him, and for Him: And He is before all things, and by Him all things consist."

GENESIS 1:27 *"So God created man in His own image, in the image of God created He him; male and female created He them."*

God didn't create man because He needed us, He created us because we need Him! If we never existed, God would still be God.

Chapter Two

Do You Have a Godly Mentor?

A MENTOR is an experienced and trusted advisor, a person who guides a less experienced person by building trust and modeling positive behaviors. A mentor will be able to teach the mentee (or student) how to do the following:

- To be committed to God.
- To take their calling seriously.
- To be a person of integrity.
- To have a consistent prayer and study life.
- To have a genuine concern for others.
- That accountability is healthy and helpful (see Romans 15:1-2, Galatians 5:25, Romans 6:2).

ROMANS 15:1-2 (NIV) *"We who are strong ought to bear with the failings of the weak and not to please ourselves. Each of us should please our neighbors for their good, to build them up."*

GALATIANS 5:25-6:2 (NKJV) *"If we live in the Spirit, let us also walk in the Spirit. Let us not become conceited, provoking one another, envying one another. Brethren, if a man is overtaken in any trespass, you who are spiritual, restore such a one in a spirit of gentleness, considering yourself lest you also be tempted."*

- A mentor will express appreciation for what you do right and will correct you when you are wrong.
- Mentoring involves bearing burdens, so others learn how to handle leadership.
- Mentoring means leading by example and encouraging your mentee or student to live what they've learned.

The Apostle Paul mentored Timothy, Titus, Silas, and Barnabas. The mentoring relationship worked because they each accepted their roles as mentor and mentee.

Elijah was a powerful and anointed Prophet of God who performed many miracles and was a mentor to Elisha. Elijah trained Elisha and was his godly mentor. Elisha had a servant's heart and was willing to humble himself, respect leadership and walk in obedience. He realized that to be a good leader, he must first be a good follower. A mentee or student must be willing to spend time focusing on the assignment given by their mentor, before qualifying for an assignment of their own.

Elisha was Elijah's assistant, and he was willing to make sacrifices to follow his mentor.

For six years Elisha served under the tutelage of Elijah and refused to leave his side. Elisha was willing to stay close to his mentor, even when times were difficult. The true essence of leadership is servitude. Elisha became like a human "sponge", eagerly soaking up all the wisdom, knowledge and anointing that he could glean from his experienced mentor, Elijah. He realized that whoever you're connected to, you'll be affected by.

Before Elijah's departure from the earth, he asked his mentee what he really desired from him. Elisha replied that he wanted a double portion of Elijah's spirit to be upon him and he received it. Elisha wound up performing twice as many miracles as his mentor Elijah!

As a mentee or student, you must be willing to admit that there are a lot of things that you don't know yet. So therefore, you must be reachable and teachable.

For example, it would not be wise to place a newborn babe in Christ over an Adult Sunday School class. Why? They need to be taught before they can teach others. We must realize that with the position, there comes accountability and responsibility. You need to be accountable to a seasoned man or woman of God. A lot of young preachers don't realize this yet. They don't fully understand that in order to walk in the anointing, you have to pay a price, you have to make sacrifices, you have to walk in the Spirit, and not get "caught up" in your flesh. So many people want the titles and the positions, but they don't want to be corrected or held accountable for their actions.

I am grateful for the tutelage that I received from one of my mentors, Pastor R.J. Brown, who walked me through my very first wedding, baptism, and funeral. I respect him because he was and is a humble and kind-hearted anointed man of God. I truly believe that we can learn a lot from our mentors.

Chapter Three

The Power of Impartation

IMPARTATION is the act of imparting something such as knowledge, wisdom or anointing. It is the transference of spiritual gifts from one anointed man or woman of God to another (for example, from Elijah to Elisha). Impartation is when the anointing seems to flow out of one person into another. Giving and receiving blessings or healings is an excellent example of the transference of gifts from one person to another, especially through the laying on of hands, and the baptism of the Holy Ghost.

Impartation Scriptures:

ACTS 2:17-18 *"And it shall come to pass in the last days, saith God, I will pour out of my Spirit upon all flesh: and your sons and daughters shall prophesy, and your young men shall see visions, and your old men shall dream dreams. And on my servants and on my handmaidens I will pour out in those days of my Spirit; and they shall prophesy."*

ACTS 1:8a *"But you shall receive power after that the Holy Ghost is come upon you..."*

ACTS 4:13 *"Now when they saw the boldness of Peter and John, and perceived that they were unlearned and ignorant men, they marvelled; and they took knowledge of them, that they had been with Jesus."*

Awesome things begin to happen when you spend time in the presence of the Lord!

ACTS 5:14-15 *"And believers were added to the Lord, multitudes both men and women. Insomuch that they brought forth the sick into the streets, and laid them on beds and couches, that at the least the shadow of Peter passing by might overshadow some of them."*

How awesome is that?! All Peter had to do was walk by, and these people were healed, because of the powerful impartation flowing out of him! If those of us who confess to be filled with the Holy Ghost walked in that type of anointing, we would put the hospitals out of business.

ACTS 19:11-12 *"And God wrought (performed) special miracles by the hands of Paul: So that from his body were brought unto the sick handkerchiefs or aprons, and the diseases departed from them, and the evil spirits went out of them."*

That's the power of the Holy Ghost in operation!

MATTHEW 5:6 *"Blessed are they which do hunger and thirst after righteousness: for they shall be filled."*

I don't know about you, but I want the Lord to fill me daily. I want Him to fill me up until I overflow. I want God to fill me with His wisdom, discernment, holy boldness, anointing, and with all the gifts and fruit of the Spirit. I want MORE of God! Reader, do you have that Holy Ghost power? You better be sure because you will be tried. Let's examine the next several verses in Acts, chapter 19.

It tells us of some pretenders, imitators, copy-cats who claimed to have miracle-working powers. Sceva, who was a Jewish chief priest, had seven sons who went around trying to cast out evil spirits, like they saw the Apostle Paul do. They would say to the demon, "In the name of Jesus whom Paul preaches, I command you to come out!" And the evil spirit answered (v 15) and said, *"Jesus I know, and Paul I know; but who are you?"* Dear reader, don't fool yourself, satan knows who you are and who you are not.

(v 16) *And the man in whom the evil spirit was leaped on them and overpowered them. The demons gave them such a beating, that they ran out of that house naked and wounded.*

The seven sons of Sceva were out of their

league. They were no match for these demonic spirits. They lacked power and authority. But when you've been endowed with Holy Ghost power, demons will have to flee. Demons recognize when a person is truly anointed, and they will tremble and must submit, because of the power in the name of JESUS.

Jesus told his disciples:

LUKE 10:19, *"Behold, I give unto you power to tread on serpents and scorpions, and over all the power of the enemy: and nothing shall by any means hurt you."*

You had better be sure you know whether or not you are equipped and empowered to battle demonic forces, or they will have you doing some crazy things, and will rip you apart like they did the sons of Sceva. Spirits are real and they will transfer from one to another.

Word of Caution: You want to make sure

that you're receiving the right kind of impartation. I've said it before, and I'll say it again: "Whoever you're connected to, you'll be affected by".

Chapter Four

How Solid is Your Foundation?

A FOUNDATION supports and anchors a building. Naturally, a house is only as solid as its foundation. A "spiritual" foundation helps to shape and develop your relationship with God. It also helps you to live your life with a greater purpose, a sense of direction, and causes you to be less stressed, because you are allowing the Lord to be the foundation of your faith.

PSALM 127:1a *"Except the Lord build the house, they labour in vain that build it."*

The Lord is a firm, steady, sure, and reliable foundation. In the natural, a foundation is a stone or concrete structure that supports a building from underneath. However, in the Spirit realm, it's important to remember that it's WHO is under the bottom that holds you up. Let me put it this way: if Jesus had not been holding you up, you would have fallen apart, and totally collapsed a long time ago.

I CORINTHIANS 3:9-17 (my paraphrase): The foundation has already been laid. If you are a child of God, then you are God's building. You are the temple of God, and the temple of God is holy. Are you holy? If you are, then don't you know that you are the temple of God, and the Spirit of God dwells in you?

MATTHEW 16:18 *"And I say also unto thee, That thou art Peter, and upon this rock I will build my church; and the gates of hell shall not prevail against it."*

II TIMOTHY 2:19 *"Nevertheless, the foundation of God standeth sure, having this seal, the Lord knows them that are his, and everyone who confesses the name of the Lord must turn away from wickedness."*

MATTHEW 7:24-27 NKJV *"Therefore whoever hears these sayings of mine and does them, I will liken him to a wise man who builds his house on a rock: and the rain descended, and the floods came and the winds blew and beat up on that house; and it did not fall, for it was founded on a rock. And everyone who hears these sayings of mine, and does not do them, will be like a foolish man who built his house on the sand: and the rain descended, the floods came, and the winds blew and beat up on that house; and it fell: and great was its fall."*

Jesus is that solid rock. Jesus is our solid foundation. On Christ, the solid rock, we must stand. All other ground is nothing but sinking sand!

Lastly, you need to check to see if you have any cracks in your spiritual foundation. Here are some signs for concern:

- If you notice you have a lack of commitment to what you've been called or assigned to do.

- If you notice that you are easily offended and it seems that you are unable to get along with others.
- If you become jealous or envious of someone else's success or blessings.
- If you notice your attitude has become increasingly negative. Keep in mind that a negative attitude will never produce positive results.

The only way to seal up those cracks in your foundation is to be honest with yourself and God. Confess your faults. Ask the Lord to help you, to deliver you, to give you strength to spend more time in prayer, devote more time in studying the Word, and build up your spiritual foundation of FAITH. I am touching and agreeing with you that every crack in your life is sealed as of today, in the name of the Father, in the name of the Son, and in the name of the Holy Ghost. Amen.

Chapter Five

Can You Handle Correction?

CORRECTION is a change to make something right, to set straight, or to remove what was wrong.

Being corrected may not feel good to you, but it can be good for you. Most people hate being corrected and will regard the person correcting them as an enemy. Often, they will receive the correction with anger and hostility. Denzel Washington says, "Some people will never like you because your spirit irritates their demons".

When we refuse correction, it opens the door to pride, anger, bitterness and unforgiveness. Refusing correction is a direct rebellion against God and those whom God has placed in authority.

PROVERBS 3:11, 12 *"My son, do not despise the*

chastening of the Lord; neither be weary of His correction: For whom the Lord loves, He corrects, just as a loving father does."

PROVERBS 15:32 *"Those who disregard discipline despise themselves, but the one who heeds correction gains understanding."*

REVELATION 3:19 (NIV) *"I correct and discipline those whom I love, so be eager to do right, and change your hearts and lives."*

There may be areas in your life that you may need to pay special attention to, such as self-control. Do you have a short fuse? Do you have a hot temper? Are you easily angered?

PSALM 37:8a *"Refrain from anger and forsake wrath."*

[ANGER is one letter away from DANGER.]

Proverbs 14:29 *"Whoever is slow to anger has great understanding, but he who has a hasty temper exalts folly"* (lacks good sense).

PROVERBS 15:1 *"A soft answer turns away*

wrath, but a harsh word stirs up anger."

PROVERBS 22:24 *"Make no friendship with a man given to anger, nor go with a wrathful man."*

Are you a "Right Fighter"? Do you get offended whenever someone tries to correct you or suggest what you should do instead? Do you always think that you're right, and hate being told that you're wrong? If someone disagrees with your opinion, do you get irritated?

Ask the Lord to reveal areas in your life where you need to practice more self-control and receive godly correction from others, without being so easily offended. After all, correction is part of our growth process. Correction is designed to make us better, not bitter.

II TIMOTHY 3:16,17 *"All Scripture is given by inspiration of God, and is profitable for doctrine, for reproof, for correction, for instruction in righteousness: That the man of God may be perfect (mature), thoroughly furnished unto all good works."*

Because many of us struggle with pride, correction can be difficult to receive. In the 18th chapter of the book of Exodus, Moses' father-in-law, Jethro, observed how Moses spent his entire day judging one case after another. This process was literally draining Moses and wearing him out. However, in love, the seasoned father-in-law, Jethro, gave Moses some godly correction.

He told Moses that his way of doing things was exhausting him and the people. He also told his son-in-law that this burden was too heavy for him to bear alone, and that he needed to delegate some of these responsibilities to qualified people. Moses needed help. Hear me when I say that it is not a sign of weakness to admit you need help. Everybody everywhere needs somebody sometime.

Moses took his father-in-law's advice without getting an attitude and, in the process, found out that his job was a lot easier and much less stressful. When correction is given in love, you can't help but receive it in love. It's not always what you say, it's how you say it!

Here is an awesome quote by Dr. Maya Angelou: "I've learned that people will forget what you said, people will forget what you did, but people will never forget how you made them feel."

Correction must be done in love to build up the person and not tear them down. If you feel you are being "led" to talk to someone about their behavior, please be certain that you are doing it for their well-being and spiritual growth, and not for your own self-righteousness. Let your correction be done in LOVE, just as Jethro did with Moses.

Here is the final scripture for this chapter:

JOB 5:17 *"Behold, happy is the man whom God corrects: therefore despise not the chastening of the Almighty."*

Chapter Six

The Gifts & Callings of God Are Without Repentance

ROMANS 11:29 *"For the gifts and callings of God are without repentance."*

This means the gifts and callings are irrevocable (won't be changed or reversed). God won't change His mind or go back on His promises. God doesn't take back the gifts He has given or disown the people He has chosen. God chose ME, because He knew one day, I would choose HIM.

JOHN 15:16a *"You have not chosen me, but I have chosen you, and ordained you, that you should go and bear fruit, and that your fruit should remain."*

I JOHN 4:19 *"We love Him, because He first loved us."*

His love for us is intentional.

Even with the "callings" on our lives, God already knew that we weren't going to dot every "i" or cross every "t". He knew we were going to do wrong, mess up, and deal with some issues and bad habits (even since some of us have been preaching). Even though you may be perfectly imperfect, God says He still has not changed His mind about you. At one time, we were all disobedient to God, but Praise the Lord, we have received MERCY (when you don't get what you really deserve) for our disobedience.

I can't speak for you, but I can say that I have messed up so many times. I have made some bad decisions, but God never gave up on me. He saw my potential and my possibilities. God knew what He had invested in me with gifts, callings, anointing, wisdom, and favor. He refused to let satan abort His plans for my life.

Fantasia sings a song entitled "Necessary". Here are some of the words to that song: "I am who I am today because God used my mistakes. He worked them for my good, like no one ever could." This song aligns so well with this scripture:

ROMANS 8:28 *"And we know that all things work together for good to them that love God, to them who are the called according to His purpose."*

I thank God for His amazing grace, and that my FLAWS have nothing to do with God's FAVOR on my life! God's PURPOSE has nothing to do with my PROBLEMS. Everything that I went through to get to where I am today, was a necessary process for me.

Some of the most anointed preachers out there have lived some "jacked up" lives, but once they let go of their sins and allowed the Lord to change them, God has used them in a great and mighty way!

ROMANS 11:29 *"For the gifts and calling of God are without repentance."*

Now I want to make it very clear that this scripture is **not** condoning our sins, nor does it give you permission to continuously sin and think that there will be no consequences for your actions. But it does offer us GRACE (when you get more than you deserve, when you miss the mark and do wrong).

ROMANS 6:12-15 *"Let not sin therefore reign in your mortal body, that you should obey it, in the lusts thereof. Do not offer any part of yourself to sin as an instrument of wickedness, but rather offer yourselves to God as those who have been brought from death to life; and offer every part of yourself to Him as an instrument of righteousness. For sin shall no longer be your master because you are not under the law, but under grace. What then? Shall we sin because we are not under the law but under grace? God forbid."*

Once you have placed your faith in God,

He will never cast you away, abandon, reject, or "ghost" you. However, as a loving Father, He will correct you and cause you to see the error of your ways, but He will never throw you away. So please, be very careful how you handle the gifts and callings on your life.

The callings on our lives are not about us. We're just God's vessels, His depositories, His royal ambassadors. We are the salt of the earth and the lights that shine in darkness.

So, let's make sure that our callings GLORIFY and not HORRIFY God by our actions and our lifestyles.

Chapter Seven

Let God Validate You

VALIDATION is the act of declaring something legally or officially acceptable or worthy. It's the act of recognizing that a person and their feelings or opinions are valid or worthwhile. It's the desire to have someone else's approval of what you say, believe or do.

Do you think that your worth as a person comes from what you do, or what you have, instead of who you are? When you allow other people to provide you with a sense of validation, you can make yourself a hostage to them.

From the very beginning of time, God himself "validated" us:

GENESIS 1:27 *"So God created man in His own image, in the image of God created He him, male and female created He them."*

Do you still need validation?

PSALM 139:14 states *"I will praise you: for I am fearfully and wonderfully made."*

In this same chapter, it tells how God knows each of us by name. He knows our heart, our thoughts, our comings, and our goings. He knows everything about us because He's omniscient (all-knowing).

LUKE 12:7b says *"We are very valuable to God."*

I PETER 2:4 (GNT) says *"Come to the Lord, the living stone rejected by people as worthless, but chosen by God as valuable."*

You are not an accident, a mistake, or a waste of space. God did not intend for you to be aborted. You matter to God. God considers you precious, priceless, and unique.

Whenever you are seeking the validation of man, remember these scriptures:

JOHN 12:43 *"For they loved the praise of men more than the praise of God."*

LUKE 6:26 *"Woe unto you when all men shall speak well of you, for so did their fathers to the false prophets."*

In other words, don't expect everyone to embrace, congratulate, receive, or even understand you. I heard the actor Denzel Washington once say this while being interviewed: "The same ones that hail you, will turn around and nail you". That's the way they were with Jesus. The same ones that cried "Hosanna", turned around and cried "Crucify!"

Popular opinion can change like the wind and when you place too much importance on it, you are just setting yourself up for disappointment.

Jesus said in MATTHEW 16:24 *"Whoever wants to be my disciple, must deny himself, and take up his cross and follow me."*

Discipleship involves self-denial, surrender, and servanthood. Many people think they are Christians because they were given the "right hand of fellowship" at church or boast because they have read the entire Bible in a year's time, or they listen to worship music regularly, or they were raised in a Christian home. Far too many people brag about being religious, but they have no relationship with Jesus!

The songwriter says, "Must Jesus bear the cross alone, and all the world go free? No, there's a cross for everyone, and there's a cross for me". Let me remind you of this truth: No cross, no crown.

Let's be honest with ourselves. Deep down we all desire to be appreciated, accepted, and even validated by others. But everyone who desires to be popular will have to choose between the approval and the validation of others and the approval and validation of God.

We're not called to try and win a popularity contest; so be careful who you put your trust in, because the devil was once an angel. When you choose to allow God to define your value, rather than people, you free yourself to follow what God has called you to do.

When GOD gets ready to validate, elevate and promote you, the opinions or approval of others is not required. When God says that it's your time or season to be blessed, no man or woman has the power or ability to stop Him from blessing you! Don't lose another night's sleep worrying about who doesn't support you or think you are valuable or worthy of being blessed; because if God is for you, it really doesn't matter who tries to be against you. I hear this in the prophetic right now: **God is up to something concerning YOU.**

The Lord is behind the scenes strategically turning your setbacks into a set-up for a miraculous comeback. You're getting ready to bounce back. God is literally preparing the hearts of people during this new season, chapter, and journey of your life, who want to bless, support and honor you, without any hidden agendas. Why? It's because they recognize the calling, gifts, favor, and the anointing upon your life.

God had to eliminate some of your unhealthy soul ties, expose the counterfeits, and cause the scales to fall from your eyes, so you could recognize your true friends as well as your "frenemies". (A frenemy is a person who pretends to be your friend when they're around you but call you everything but a child of God behind your back,)

These new people that God has positioned to be in your life will want to participate in your success because they know that the favor of God and the hand of God is resting mightily upon you.

When God validates you, you have the Most High orchestrating your every move; and He will pour out blessings upon you, so you can bless others!

Now, I think it's time for a PRAISE BREAK!

Chapter Eight

Have You Really Been Transformed?

Our minds must be renewed daily or we will do a lot of "stinking thinking". Renewing your mind means changing the way you think to create a better life for yourself, as well as a life that honors God.

PHILIPPIANS 2:5 *"Let this mind be in you, which was also in Christ Jesus."*

ISAIAH 26:3 *"He will keep you in perfect peace, when your mind is stayed on Him, because you trust in Him."*

TRANSFORMATION means having a change of heart. Tamela Mann sings a song that says, "Change me Oh God, make me more like You. Change me Oh God, wash me through and through."

Just like we put our clothes in the washing machine and rinse them to make sure they're clean, we must be washed as well. David said in PSALM 51:10 *"Create in me a clean heart, O God; and renew a right spirit within me."*

Precious Reader, we've got to have an inside job. We must be changed/transformed from the inside out.

EZEKIEL 36:26 (NIV) *"I will give you a new heart and put a new spirit in you; I will remove from you your heart of stone and give you a heart of flesh."*

Let me use myself as an example. I haven't forgotten how to curse, I'm just more careful about the words that come out of my mouth. I've heard many Christians say that if they think it, they might as well speak it. Not so! Let me back this up with God's Word:

PROVERBS 25:28 states: *"The person that has no rule or control over their own spirit, is like a city that is broken down, and without walls."*

Paul says in II CORINTHIANS 10:5b *"That we are to bring every thought into captivity to the obedience of Christ."*

MATTHEW 15:11 *"It's not that which goes into the mouth that defiles a man, but that which comes out of the mouth, this defiles a man."*

EPHESIANS 4:29a *"Let no corrupt communication proceed out of your mouth."*

Put a filter on your tongue. The Holy Ghost is a tongue tamer. Some of the places I used to hang out in, back in the day, are still in existence. I pass by them on a frequent basis, but I no longer have a desire to go in there anymore. Why? Because I have been TRANSFORMED. The things I used to do; I don't do them anymore. The places I used to go; I don't go there anymore. A change has come over me.

II CORINTHIANS 5:17 *"Therefore if any man be in Christ, he is a new creature, old things are passed away; behold all things are become **new**."*

When you've truly been transformed (from the inside out), you will never be the same again!

MATTHEW 23:25-26 *"Woe unto you, scribes and Pharisees, hypocrites! for you clean the outside of the cup and of the platter, but within they are full of greed and self-indulgence. You are spiritually blind. First clean the inside of the cup and platter, that the outside of them may be clean also."*

Don't be dressed up on the OUTSIDE but messed up on the INSIDE.

ROMANS 12:1 *"I beseech you therefore brethren, by the mercies of God, that you present your bodies a living sacrifice, holy, acceptable unto God, which is your reasonable service."*

The word "holy" is not talking about a particular denomination or wearing a long dress or skirt, no jewelry, no makeup, or women not wearing pants, or having braided hair. True holiness is a consecrated, surrendered, and dedicated way of life.

ROMANS 12:2 *"And be not conformed to this world but be ye transformed by the renewing of your mind."*

Let me make this plain: going to church doesn't make you a Christian any more than sitting in a garage makes you a car. The best evidence of being a Christian is to B1.

Believe me when I say this: everyone in your circle won't be happy about your true transformation. You're not made to be included in everybody's circle. It's not about how many Facebook friends you have, because everybody is not who they post to be anyway. It's not about being noticed, approved, accepted, received, or included by man, but it is about your personal and intimate relationship with Jesus Christ, since you have been transformed.

You may lose some people in your transformation process, but the rapper

Casanova sums it up so well, when he says: "People don't abandon people they love, they abandon people they were using. Don't be afraid of losing people, be afraid of losing yourself."

When you've truly been transformed, you will no longer desire to be a PEOPLE PLEASER, your heart's desire will long to be a GOD PLEASER.

Chapter Nine

How Dedicated Are You?

Have you counted the cost?

LUKE 14:33 Jesus says, *"Whoever among you that doesn't forsake all he has, cannot be my disciple"* (follower).

Being a follower of Jesus Christ involves DEDICATION. We can't follow Jesus and the ways of the world at the same time. Following Christ may cost us some relationships, material things or even our life. In Jesus' earthly ministry, there came a time when supportive public opinion turned vicious, and cheering crowds became jeering crowds. When we become one of His disciples, we no longer belong to this world. (We are *in* the world, but not *of* the world).

When we choose to follow Jesus, we release control of our lives. True dedication doesn't come from what you do occasionally, it comes from what you do consistently.

I CORINTHIANS 10:21 "*You cannot drink the cup of the Lord, and the cup of the devils: you cannot be partakers of the Lord's table, and of the table of the devils.*" In other words, you can't serve God with one foot under two tables!

I CORINTHIANS 9:27 (NLT) "*I discipline my body like an athlete, training it to do what it should. Otherwise, I fear that after preaching to others, I myself might be a castaway*" (considered unfit or disqualified).

I don't know about you, but I don't want my living, my teaching or preaching to be in vain. I want to be a **doer** of the Word. I want my WALKING to do my TALKING. I want others to be able to see Jesus living in me. Afterall, people may not believe what I *say* I do, but they will believe what they *see* me do!

MATTEW 6:24 "*No man can serve two masters; for either he will hate the one and love the other; or else he will be devoted to the one and despise the other, you cannot serve God and mammon"* (false object of worship and devotion).

Serving TWO is hard to DO. Our hearts are not designed to serve two masters. We can't straddle the fence and call ourselves dedicated.

ACTS 26:28 *"King Agrippa said unto the Apostle Paul, Almost thou persuaded me to be a Christian."*

The R&B singer Brandy has a song entitled, "Almost Doesn't Count." What is holding you back from being fully committed?

I KINGS 18:21 *"The Prophet Elijah went before the people and said, 'How long will you halt* (be undecided) *between two opinions? If the Lord is God, follow Him; but if Baal* (an idol god)*, then follow him', but the people said nothing."*

Dear Reader, what's your honest response to this question?

JOSHUA 24:15 *"And if it seem evil unto you to serve the Lord, choose ye this day whom you will serve; but as for me and my house, we will serve the Lord."*

The same choice is ours today. However, we must keep in mind that our choices in life have consequences. God wants to be a priority in our lives, not an afterthought.

MATTEW 22:37-38 Jesus says, *"Love the Lord with* ***all*** *your heart, and with* ***all*** *your soul, and with* ***all*** *your mind. This is the first and great commandment"* (emphasis mine).

I would like to share this short story about DEDICATION: There was a farmer who fell on hard times financially. He had three precious animals who loved him and wanted to help in his time of need: a chicken, a cow, and a pig. The chicken decided she would donate a dozen of her fresh brown eggs. They make delicious cakes. The cow decided she would donate a gallon of fresh milk. A glass of milk would be great with a big slice of cake. Then, the cow and the chicken looked at the pig and said, "What are you going to give?" The pig said, "I can't give just a part of me, it's ALL or nothing at all!"

Are you as committed as this pig? Are you willing to give God your ALL, your BEST, your ONLY, your LAST, withholding NOTHING? Are you truly dedicated to God's will and His way for your life? If you're serious about being fully dedicated, then pray this prayer out loud: "Heavenly Father, I thank you for blessing me with all my gifts, talents, skills, and abilities. I dedicate them all to you to be used for your glory and to be a blessing to others. Amen."

I would like to end this chapter with a quote by Dr. Martin Luther King Jr.: "Use me, God. Show me how to take who I am, who I want to be, and what I can do, and use it for a purpose greater than myself."

Chapter Ten

Have You Ever Been Told You Have a Calling on Your Life?

There's a gift related CALLING on your life that God placed inside of you before you were ever born. It stays with you and it manifests in different ways during different seasons of your life. It must be identified, developed, and nourished. FYI: everyone who is called is not necessarily called to be a preacher.

PSALM 1:3a *"The blessed person is like a tree planted by the rivers of water, that brings forth his fruit in his season; his leaf* (work) *also shall not wither; and whatsoever they do shall prosper."* In other words, yield **your** fruit.

- If you've been called to preach…then preach.

- If you've been called to teach…then teach.
- If you've been called to sing…then sing.
- If writing is your calling…then start writing.
- If your calling is designing…then get your creative juices flowing.
- You're only responsible to produce what's inside of YOU.

A tree is known by the fruit it bears, for every tree is known by its own fruit. What God speaks over your life will bear fruit in the right season. We're all called to do something in life.

God will never force anyone to respond to His calling against their will. He's too much of a gentleman to do that. Your calling is how God created you to serve, honor, worship and give Him glory in everything that you do.

Your calling is the destiny upon your life.

ROMANS 8:28 *"And we know that all things*

*work together for good, to those who love God, to those who are the **called** according to His purpose"* (emphasis mine).

God gives specific gifts (callings) to specific people for a specific purpose or plan. All gifts are uniquely designed and assigned by God.

Responding to God's call is a process that requires time, maturity, patience, prayer, and a willingness to submit to God's will and His ways over your life. When there's a true calling upon your life, satan will try every trick in his book to try and convince you that God can't or won't use you, call you, bless you, or forgive you, because of your past. However, the devil is a liar!

The Bible says in I JOHN 1:4 *"If we confess our faults (sins), He is faithful and just to forgive us and will cleanse us from all unrighteousness."*

Many of our greatest anointings come after our greatest challenges. When God calls you, how will you respond? Will you offer excuses like Moses did in EXODUS 4:10, because he was fearful and had a speech impediment? Disability does not mean inability. God reassured Moses that He would be with him. And God will be with you as well. When God calls you, will you be like Jonah, and try to run and hide (see JONAH 1:1-3)?

PSALM 139:7-8 says: *"Where shall I go from your spirit, or how can I flee from your presence? If I ascend up into heaven, you are there: if I make my bed in hell, behold, you are there."* That's because the Lord is omnipresent. He's able to be all places at the same time.

Or will you say, "Here I am Lord. You know all about my issues, faults, imperfections, limitations, and my insecurities; but if you still choose to call me and use me despite myself, Lord I surrender. Let your will be done in my life, use me for your glory."

FYI: When God calls you, He already knows everything about you because He's omniscient (all-knowing). He knows what you're capable of doing. If you follow God's leading, He will do the work in you so you can do what He's called you to do. Not only does God want to use you and bless you, but He wants to bless others through you. Sometimes the things that we think are our greatest flaws can be the very things that God uses for His greatest glory. If God calls you, He will anoint you to do what He's called you to do. Man's extremities are God's opportunities.

You may not feel qualified to do anything special but remember this: God doesn't always call the **qualified**, but He always qualifies the **called**. II TIMOTHY 1:8b-9 (my paraphrase) "The power of God has saved us, and called us with a holy calling, not according to our works, but according to His own purpose and grace, which was given to us in Christ Jesus **before** the world began."

ISAIAH 43:1b states *"Fear not: for I have*

redeemed you, I have called you by your name: you are mine."

Tasha Cobbs Leonard sings a song that says, "He knows my name". Others may forget all about you, but not God!

PHILIPPIANS 3:14 *"I press toward the mark for the prize of the high calling of God in Christ Jesus."*

In the book of I SAMUEL in the 16th chapter, we read about a time when God was ready to anoint the next king of Israel. He sent the prophet Samuel to Jesse's house. Seven of Jesse's sons came and stood before Samuel, waiting for his approval, but the Lord rejected all of them! Even though they looked the part, the calling and the anointing was NOT upon their lives for this specific assignment!

We can be dressed up on the outside, but so messed up on the inside. The Lord told the prophet Samuel that *man looks at the* ***outward appearance****, but God looks on the* ***heart.*** After seven rejections from the Lord, Samuel asked Jesse if he had any more sons. Jesse responded that he had one more son, the youngest, who was out in the fields, tending the sheep. Samuel said, *"Send and fetch him: for we won't sit down until he comes"*.

Dear Reader, have you ever considered that God may have somebody somewhere, waiting on **your** arrival, waiting on your unique anointing, waiting on you to respond to the calling upon your life? We don't hear the word "fetch" much in this day and time. FETCH simply means to go after, go and bring back. Now before any of you get too spiritually deep… there was a time when God had to fetch us out. He fetched some of us out of the night clubs, out of crack houses, out of dens of depression, and out of promiscuous lifestyles. If we had not been fetched out, we would still be in bondage and shackles.

When God was about to call Paul for ministry, he told a disciple named Ananias to go and lay his hands on Paul so he could receive his sight. Ananias began telling the Lord about all the evil things that Paul was doing; especially persecuting the people of God. But our loving God told Ananias to go and do what he was told to do. In other words, God was telling Ananias to stay in his lane. God considered Paul a **chosen vessel,** even before his conversion. You can read about this in ACTS 9:10-15.

News Flash: there might be someone in your life who is making accusations about you and against you, assassinating your character, and forever bringing up your past. Let's be honest, some of the things they're saying about you may be true, but thank God, your **history** does not determine your **destiny.** Here is biblical proof:

II CORINTHIANS 5:17 *"Therefore if* ***any*** *man be in Christ, he is a new creature: old things are passed away; behold* ***all*** *things are become new"* (emphasis mine).

I recently had a conversation with my hair stylist concerning her calling to do hair. She shared how she started shampooing heads for a licensed cosmetologist. She would observe her talents and eventually she had a desire to go to Beauty School. Now she owns her own salon, is very creative and quite successful. Over the years she has perfected her gifts and calling; but it was a process. Someone had to take the time to invest in her, show her "the ropes", and pour into her life. That person who trained my stylist was able to see the inner gifts and talents in her life before she did. My stylist strives to make every woman feel and look more beautiful when we leave her salon.

In case you didn't know: your **career** is what you paid for. Your **calling** is what you're **made for.** God will equip you with everything you need to perform the calling on your life!

Chapter Eleven

Separation is Required (You Need Some "Me" Time)

SEPARATION is defined as a time of isolation, to be set apart, disconnected, and removed from. There are times when it will be necessary to separate yourself from the crowds, the distractions, and the noise.

II CORINTHIANS 6:17a *"Wherefore come out from among them, and be ye separate, saith the Lord."*

God didn't call us out to fit in or blend in. He called us out, to stand out.

MARK 1:35 *"And in the morning, rising up a great while before day, Jesus went out, and departed into a solitary place, and there prayed."*

Jesus separated himself and went to a secret place, without any distractions, so he could pray.

LUKE 6:12 tells us that Jesus spent all night praying on a mountain before choosing his twelve disciples. This is an excellent example of Jesus' need for prayer before making life changing decisions. As his followers, we need to pray before making important decisions.

PROVERBS 3:6 tells us *"In all thy ways acknowledge Him, and He shall direct thy paths,"*

LUKE 5:15, 16 *"But so much the more went there a fame abroad of Him: and great multitudes came together to hear, and to be healed of their infirmities. And He withdrew himself into the wilderness and prayed."* Why? Because people can drain your anointing. If it was necessary for Jesus to get away from the crowds and have some "me time" (or some time alone) with the Heavenly Father, then it must be mandatory for us to do the same.

Learn to be okay with not being invited, considered, or included in other people's circles. Sometimes, that just might be God's way of shielding and protecting you. Everybody and everything are not meant for you.

When people don't see you or hear your name mentioned for quite a while, they tend to make assumptions, such as: you must have backslidden, or God is no longer using you. But what they don't know is that God has you on a spiritual hiatus/sabbatical, and it is necessary for you to be in spiritual isolation for a season.

What they don't have a clue about is that God is preparing you for a brand-new level of anointing. He's giving you keener sensitivity to His still small voice. He's taking your ministry to a brand-new dimension. He's doing a new thing in you! God is elevating you. Elevation requires separation.

It's so important that you make time to get into the presence of the Lord. When you get into the presence of the Lord, He will reveal things that you need to know. He will explain things and He will make divine deposits into your spirit and give you a peace that passes all understanding.

Separation can also include a pruning process. You'll never get all that God wants you to have if you stay connected to the things or people you need to let go of!

JOHN 15:1-2 *"I am the true vine, and my Father is the husbandman* (vinedresser). *Every branch in me that bears no fruit he takes away: and every branch that bears fruit, he purges it, that it may bring forth more fruit."*

We must decide what needs to stay or go in our lives. We must determine if it is helping or hindering our growth. We may need to get rid of some unhealthy habits or some toxic relationships; because remember "whoever we're connected to, we'll be affected by". Are there things or people in your life that are stunting your growth and taking up valuable time that you need to be spending in the presence of God? Ask yourself if these things or people are worth holding on to.

Beloved, there are some things and people that you simply can't take into your next season or chapter. It's true that you must meet people where they are, and sometimes you must leave them there. YOU must determine who is your **fountain** and who is your **drain**.

Your fountain is that person who charges your spiritual battery, who builds you up by speaking positive words of encouragement. Your drain is that person who seems to zap the strength and life out of you with their constant negativity and complaining. You are more excited to see them going, than you are to see them coming.

ME TIME: You need some aloneness time. You need some time alone to reflect. You need some QUIET time. You need some **peace,** so you won't fall to **pieces**. If you constantly give, give, give, go, go, go, and do, do, do, you can easily get lost in the process. Please don't lose yourself in the process of always trying to help others.

We all make choices, but in the end, our choices make us. Our choices can alter our lives forever. We have to know our limits and we also have to set boundaries. We have to know when to say "No", and not beat ourselves up by feeling guilty. Take it from me, your "no" can be an opportunity for someone else to say "yes". Sometimes you have to say "no" to others, so you can say "yes" to yourself. You're not meant to do it all. In fact, you're not built to do it all.

We really do teach people how to treat us. The more you do, the more people expect you to do. When we try to become everything to everybody, we get lost in the process. We become so consumed with doing so much for others, that we fail to take proper care of ourselves. There's only one of you.

I used to think people were being selfish saying they were taking some "me time", but

I found out the hard way that I need to be kind to myself. I do so much for others, I need to invest some time in me. I matter. I'm important. I'm valuable. I'm a priority. So now I treat myself to a nice lunch, a mani-pedi, buy myself a gift, go for a work-out or just relax; and it feels good!

My husband and my doctors tell me all the time that I can't take care of others if I don't learn to take care of myself. We can try to multi-task and wear many hats, doing so many things, even in the church. But I've learned from experience, that we can become so busy doing things **for** Jesus, that we don't have quality time to spend **with** Jesus. Now "marinate" on that for a while.

If you're trying to burn the candle from both ends, stop it, because it will leave you exhausted, burned out, worn out, drained, depleted and stressed out! Hear me when I say that **stress** will **mess** you up! Many times, stress comes from trying to do it all on your own.

If you're feeling overwhelmed, your body is giving you a signal that it needs to take a break and slow down. You need to relax, relate, and release. You need to get away. You may need a day-cation or a day at the spa. You don't have an "S" on your chest! You may need a spiritual and emotional overhaul.

MATTHEW 11:28 *"Come unto me, all ye that labour and are heavy laden, and I will give you rest."*

You're trying to wear too many hats. You're trying to be too many things to too many people. This verse is saying, "Come and let me build you up again. Come and let me restore you and refresh you. Come and let me recharge your spiritual battery."

You can't afford to procrastinate any longer. You need this "me time". This is a reservation without the privilege of cancellation. You are a priority. Shut your phone down. No texting. No emails. No TV. You need this one-on-one time with the Lord. No distractions. No interruptions. Just Jesus and you. Begin to call on that great name. Let Him know that you can't afford to wait another second of another minute of another hour. You need that alone time, that intimate time alone with God, where you can be real and transparent, naked, and not ashamed.

Right where you are, just throw up both of your hands and say, "Lord, I need you. Lord, whatever you want to do in my life, I surrender my will. Lord, I realize if I'm too busy to spend time with You, then I am way too busy! Lord, today I choose to make you my number one priority. Lord, I need You to survive. I can't make it without You. Lord, forgive me for all the decisions I made without getting your approval first. Amen."

Chapter Twelve

Appreciation (Do You Have an Attitude of Gratitude?)

I personally believe that we all want to be appreciated, celebrated, and not just tolerated. The Bible gives us a perfect example of showing appreciation to God in these verses:

PSALM 103: 2-5 *"Bless the Lord, O my soul, and forget not all His benefits: Who forgives all our iniquities; who heals all our diseases; who redeems our life from destruction; who crowns us with lovingkindness and tender mercies; who satisfies our mouth with good things."*

PSALM 68:19 *"Blessed be the Lord, who daily loads us with benefits"* (blessings).

PSALM 150:6 *"Let everything that has breath praise the Lord. Praise ye the Lord."*

Dear Reader, if you're still breathing, then

you owe God a praise. We should be appreciative and grateful that the Lord chose to wake us up this morning and start us on our way. He didn't have to do it, but aren't you glad He did? Beloved, gratitude is an attitude. Do you have an attitude of gratitude? Or do you take your blessings for granted? Let me make this very plain: God doesn't owe us anything, but we owe Him everything.

I THESSALONIANS 5:18 *"Give thanks in all things, for this is the will of God in Christ Jesus concerning you."*

My mother always taught me when somebody does something nice for you, the least you can do is say, "Thank you!" Here are a few ways of saying thank you and showing appreciation in different languages:

French	Merci
German	Danke
Portuguese	Obrigado
Spanish	Gracias

Indonesian	Terima Kasih
Italian	Grazie
Vietnamese	Camon
Japanese	Arigato
Swahili	Asante

Remember that actions speak louder than words. Try doing some intentional acts of kindness, such as mailing a "Just Because" card or a letter of encouragement to a friend who may be going through a difficult time. Perhaps you could treat a friend or neighbor with physical challenges to a mani-pedi. It would be a nice gesture to offer to babysit for new parents or take a friend out to lunch who recently lost a loved one. Sometimes a few kind words can really brighten someone's day. You might be surprised how great it would make a person feel to hear you say, "I'm thankful and blessed to have you in my life", or "You inspire me to pursue greatness". Other intentional acts of kindness might include slowing down and allowing someone else to merge into traffic or letting someone ahead of you in line at the grocery store or offering to pay for a meal for a first responder or a soldier.

The Good Samaritan in LUKE 10:25-37 stopped to help a man who had been robbed, beaten, and left for dead. This was after a priest and a Levite passed him by. Everybody everywhere needs somebody sometime.

Mother Teresa says, "I can do things you cannot. You can do things I cannot. Together we can do great things."

I publicly want to acknowledge and appreciate all the people who were there for me at different seasons in my life. Some of you were there when I had my mountaintop experiences, and others stood by me when I was at my weakest and lowest points. I realize that I didn't get to where I am today on my own, it took a village to sustain me. That village supported me, pushed me, encouraged me, challenged me, poured into my life when I was broke, busted, and disgusted. Through it all, you didn't give up on me, you saw the best in me, and I sincerely want you to know that I am truly grateful, much obliged, and from the bottom of my heart, I thank you and I APPRECIATE all that you've ever done on my behalf. May our Heavenly Father multiply your blessings!

Chapter Thirteen

Are You Contaminated?

CONTAMINATION is making or being made impure by polluting or poisoning. It is causing something to be unsuitable, unclean, and causes harm by being in contact with. A spiritual contamination is anything that would cause a person to become spiritually unclean. It's a heart thing.

MATTHEW 15:18 *"Those things which proceed out of the mouth come from the heart; and they defile* (contaminate) *the man."*

JEREMIAH 17:9-10 *"The heart is deceitful above all things, and desperately wicked: who can know it? I the Lord search the heart, I try the reins, even to give every man according to his ways, and according to the fruit of his doings."*

That's why the Psalmist David found it necessary to say in PSALM 51:10 *"Create in me a clean heart, O God, and renew a right spirit within me."*

Beloved, could there be some things in your heart that might need cleansing?

JEALOUSY can contaminate a person's heart. In the 26th chapter of GENESIS, starting at verse 12, it tells how the Lord greatly blessed Abraham's son, Isaac. The Philistines were so jealous that they threw dirt into his wells, contaminating them. They were mudslingers. Mudslingers will spread things against your character and slander your name to others for no apparent reason.

There may be some modern-day Philistines who are jealous of you and are trying to sling dirt/mud into your spiritual wells. They are threatened by the anointing and the favor of God upon your life. But if God is for you, man or woman of God, hear me when I say that absolutely **no weapon** formed against you shall have the ability to prosper. They just won't work. They may be formed, but they won't work.

In I SAMUEL 18:6-11 we see that after David killed the giant Goliath and the women of the nearby cities were celebrating his victory, King Saul became extremely angry and jealous. He even plotted to kill David more than once. But God protected David.

Dear Reader, please don't allow jealousy to **contaminate** your heart. What God has for you, it is for YOU. If your heart is right with God, He has a blessing with your name on it.

Your heart can also be contaminated with UNFORGIVENESS, BITTERNESS, HATRED, or the like. This is a Scripture that deals with contamination of the heart:

PROVERBS 18:19 *"A brother offended is harder to be won than a strong city: and their contentions are like the bars of a castle."*

This scripture is talking about a brother or sister, claiming to be a child of God. But when that same child of God feels as though you have offended them, they become angry and don't want to hear anything else that you have to say. It would be easier for you to get through to the bars of a fortified castle, than it would be for you to get through to their stony heart. It really shouldn't be that way between Christians. We are supposed to walk in love and forgiveness. We should be able to disagree without being disagreeable.

If you are intent on holding on to an offense, you may need to have a spiritual heart transplant surgery to remove all the **contamination** that is in your heart. The Lord Himself is the best cardiologist on the planet. Here's what He's able to do:

EZEKIAL 36:26-27 *"A new heart also will I give you, and a new spirit will I put within you: and I will take away the stony heart out of your flesh, and I will give you a heart of flesh. And I will put my spirit within you, and cause you to walk in my statutes, and you shall keep my judgments, and do them."*

Whoever it is or whatever it is, don't let them or it contaminate your heart any longer. Don't expect positive changes in your life if you constantly surround yourself with negative people, because bad company corrupts good character. Beloved, you can't change the people around you, but you can change the people you choose to be around.

OFFENSE IS A BLESSING BLOCKER.

Chapter Fourteen

Don't Be So Quick to Try and Judge Others

To JUDGE means to criticize or form an opinion about something or someone.

MATTHEW 7:1-5 (NIV) *"Do not judge, or you will be judged. For in the same way you judge others, you will be judged, and with the measure you use, it will be measured to you. Why do you look at the speck of sawdust in your brother's eye and pay no attention to the plank in your own eye? How can you say to your brother, Let me take the speck out of your eye, when all the time there's a plank in your own eye? You hypocrite, first take the plank out of your own eye, and then you will see clearly to remove the speck from your brother's eye."*

There's a song by the William Brothers that says, "Sweep around your own front door, before you try and sweep around mine."

Picture this demonstration in your mind: there's a sheet of paper with a lot of lines on it. On each line, there are pictures of all the good things that you've ever done in your life. But, amid all those good things, there is one tiny dot. That tiny dot represents the one wrong thing that you did in your life, that thing that some people will never let you forget. Regardless of all the good things that you've done since then, there will always be a person who will choose to focus on your wrong. But Beloved, if you repented of your wrongdoing, God forgave you, and threw that sin into the sea of forgetfulness to be remembered no more! So don't you dare allow any self-righteous judgmental, mean-spirited people cause you to live in **condemnation,** because whom the Son sets free, is free indeed (see JOHN 8:36)!

Judging a person does not define who **they** are, it defines who **you** are. Be very careful before you try and judge another person. Fix yourself first. Take a moment and check your own shortcomings and you may find that you're not as perfect as you think you are. Your beliefs don't make you a better person, your behavior does. Dr. Maya Angelou says, "When someone shows you who they are, believe them the first time". I say, "People may not believe what you **say** you do, but they will believe what they **see** you do".

Do you consider it judging a person if they call themselves an apple tree, but all you ever see on their tree are pecans so you call them a pecan tree? The Bible says a tree is known by the fruit it bears. Don't be so easily deceived because sugar and salt look the same. I have seen people with Christian bumper stickers on the back of their vehicles; yet some of those same people drive around full of road rage, yelling out their windows to the top of their lungs, honking their horns like maniacs and flipping you the "bird". Let me be bold enough to say this: If you don't have genuine Christian love on the inside of you, your Christian bumper sticker isn't going to impress anybody.

Sometimes we're guilty of trying to judge someone else's destiny or outcome based on their current condition or season. Here are some examples:

One season Hannah was in the temple weeping, the next season she was in the temple rejoicing.

One season Saul was persecuting the Christians, the next season he was preaching the gospel of Jesus Christ.

One season the woman at the well was labeled promiscuous, the next season she was evangelizing (running into the city to tell the people, "Come see a man!").

One season Job lost all his children, livestock, and servants, the next season he ended up with twice as much as he had before. (He received double for all his trouble.)

Marinate on this: Your troubles have an expiration date. Your troubles won't last forever. Your **condition** is not your **conclusion**. What you start with is not what you're stuck with. So don't make a permanent decision based on a temporary condition or season.

Motivational speaker Les Brown says, "When something bad happens to you, you have three choices. You can either let it define you, let it destroy you, or you can let it strengthen you". Other people's opinion of you does not have to become your reality. Baby, it's not what they call you, it's what you answer to.

JENNIFER HUDSON

In 2004, Jennifer Hudson competed in season three of the popular television series, American Idol and was eliminated, placing at number seven. She was voted off after Judge Simon Cowell told her, "You're out of your depth in this competition". Hudson later admitted that she cried all the next day because hearing those words hurt. During another season of Jennifer's life, in 2008, she tragically lost her mother, brother and her 7-year-old nephew at the diabolical hands of her brother-in-law, which of course left her totally devastated!

Despite her American Idol loss, Jennifer Hudson (J-Hud) is now regarded as one of the most successful contestants in the show's history. She has achieved "EGOT" status (she's won Emmy, Grammy, Oscar, and Tony Awards). She has also received NAACP and Golden Globe awards. She has a star on the Hollywood Walk of Fame, has performed on Broadway and has her own TV show. J-Hud's seasons changed and so can yours!

People are always going to talk; but your times are in God's hands. Don't you dare place a period where God has placed a comma. It ain't over till God says it's over. Your best is yet to come! There's a NEXT to your chapter/season.

Chapter Fifteen

Learn To Be a Real Seeker of God

To SEEK means to chase after, to pursue.

Gospel artist Vashawn Mitchell sings a song that says: "I'm chasing after you, no matter what I have to do, cause I need you more and more".

MARK 1:35 *"And in the morning, rising up a great while before day, Jesus went out and departed into a solitary place, and there prayed."*

This verse is not necessarily saying that you must get up at 4 or 5 o'clock in the morning. But it means early in the morning, when you first wake up, **before** you try and plan your busy day, let God order your steps and direct your paths. Spend quality time in His presence and listen to His still small voice. If you listen for His instructions, you will succeed at what He calls you to do.

PROVERBS 8:17 *"I love them that love me; and those that seek me early shall find me."*

ARE YOU A REAL SEEKER OR A THRILL SEEKER?

A **real seeker** wants more of an intimate and personal relationship with Jesus. A **thrill seeker** seeks God for selfish reasons, such as wanting more gifts, blessings, and excitement.

PSALM 42:1 *"As the hart* (deer) *pants after the water brooks, so pants my soul after thee, O' God"*.

In other words, I realize that water is essential, and I don't want to be spiritually dehydrated, so I admit that I need you to survive!

LAMENTATIONS 3:25: *"The Lord is good unto them that wait for Him, to the soul that seeks Him."*

HEBREWS 11:6 *"But without faith it is impossible to please Him: for he that cometh to*

God must believe that He is, and that He is a rewarder of them that diligently seek Him." The more we **seek** and **depend on** God, the more our problems decrease and our peace will increase.

ARE YOU SEEKING GOD'S HAND OR HIS FACE?

PSALM 27:8 "When *you say, Seek my face; my heart said unto you, your face, Lord will I seek*".

Are you seeking after the gifts, or the Giver of the gifts? When you need help deciding what to do, or which way to go, seek God first.

PROVERBS 3:5-6 *"Trust in the Lord with all your heart; and lean not unto your own understanding. In all your ways acknowledge Him, and He shall direct your paths."*

What are you desiring, seeking, or chasing after? Are you seeking after fame, fortune, popularity, special recognition, or attention?

MATTHEW 6:33: *"But seek ye **first** the Kingdom*

of God and His righteousness; and all these things shall be added unto you" (emphasis mine).

Make sure your priorities are in order. David said in PSALM 27:4 *"One thing have I desired of the Lord, that will I seek after; that I may dwell in the house of the Lord all the days of my life, to behold the beauty of the Lord, and to enquire* (seek) *in His temple."*

What is the ONE thing you desire from God more than anything else? What or who is filling the void in your life?

ROMANS 8:35 *"Who shall separate you from the love of Christ?"*

Sometimes we stray away from God because of wrong associations who hinder us from seeking the Lord.

In I KINGS the 11th chapter, the Bible says that *"King Solomon loved many strange women who turned his heart after other gods… and his heart was not perfect with the Lord his God, as was the heart of David his father."*

When we depart from God, that means we are **outside** of His will. When we depart from God, it separates us from God. It is mandatory that we learn to seek God.

PSALM 119:10 *"With my whole heart have I sought thee: O' let me not wander from your commandments"*.

Seeking the Lord means seeking His presence.

II CHRONICLES 7:14 *"If my people, which are called by my name, shall humble them- selves and pray, and seek my face, and turn from their wicked ways; then will I hear from heaven, and will forgive their sin, and will heal their land."*

This means that we must be in a state of **humility** to seek God. Beloved, we cannot seek the Lord until we humble ourselves and pray first. We must be willing to decrease for the Lord to increase in our lives; that means less of us, and more of Him.

JEREMIAH 29:13 *"You will seek me and find me*

when you seek me with all of your heart" (withholding nothing).

Here's a word of CAUTION:

II CHRONICLES 15:2b *"The Lord is with you, while you be with Him; and if you shall seek Him, He will be found of you; but if you forsake Him, He will forsake you."*

PSALM 63:1 *"O God, you are my God; early will I seek you: my soul thirsts for you, my flesh longs for you in a dry and thirsty land, where there is no water."*

This verse is not just talking about seeking the Lord early in the morning, but it also means seeking the Lord early on amid your trouble or situation before things get totally out of control. In other words, don't wait until you're up to your neck in trouble before you seek the Lord.

PSALM 34:4 *"I sought the Lord and He heard me and delivered me from all my fears."* That includes fears of failure, loneliness, rejection, sickness....

PSALM 9:10 *"And they that know your name will put their trust in you: for you Lord, have not forsaken them that seek you."*

ISAIAH 55:6 *"Seek ye the Lord while He may be found; call on Him while He is near."*

David gave this charge to his son Solomon in I CHRONICLES 28:9 *"And you Solomon my son, know the God of your father, and serve Him with a perfect heart and with a willing mind: for the Lord searches all hearts, and understands all the imaginations of the thoughts: if you seek Him, He will be found of you: but if you forsake Him, He will cast you off forever."*

Nobody else's relationship with God can take the place of your relationship with God. Let me end this chapter by saying, "If you are too busy to spend time with God, then you are much too busy! You need to learn to seek God early.

Chapter Sixteen

Should There Be Competition in The Body of Christ?

First, let's get a clear definition of the word COMPETITION. It is an event or contest in which people compete. Competition is also the state of trying to defeat or be more successful than another. It is where one person's victory is another person's loss. Competition is often considered to be the opposite of cooperation, collaboration, or partnership. Simply put, it means having a strong desire to win or be the best. Competition is a "spirit" and it has a lot to do with the attitude of the heart.

Let me say that it's only natural to want to do your very best, at what you've been called or assigned to do.

In the world, there are all sorts of competitions such as sporting events, debates, beauty, and cooking contests, and even the battle of the bands. I'm not saying that ALL competition is bad; but it becomes a problem when it borders on being excessive and mean-spirited. Sadly, the spirit of competition is in the church today. I've witnessed overly competitive choirs, musicians, praise dancers, and even preachers who are literally trying to prove that they can "out-preach" someone else. I personally feel that this spirit should NOT be celebrated or tolerated in the Body of Christ.

It's true, we're ***in*** the world, but we're not ***of*** the world. We have people arguing and competing over titles, positions, who has more degrees, or who attended the most prestigious universities. There are pastors who are bragging over who has the most members, who has more Facebook followers and who has the largest and the newest sanctuaries. Let me not forget to add those preachers who feel they're more anointed than others, or who have more speaking engagements on their calendars, or who has the latest model cars, or who has their own private jet. This sounds like a lot of EGO to me (Edging God Out).

Is it just my feeling, or does there seem to be a lot of JEALOUSY among preachers? There are far too many people in the Body of Christ who are trying to "keep up with the Jones'". That's when you try and prove that you're just as good and successful as other people, by getting what they have and doing what they do.

This spirit of competition will have you purchasing things you know you can't afford. You wind up spending more than you make, because you're trying to fake it, until you make it. In other words, you're trying to live a "filet mignon" lifestyle on a "burger budget". Let me tell you this in love: Live within your means and stop trying to keep up with the Jones'. Besides, you don't know what the Jones' had to do to get what they've got, or what they must do to try and keep it. Baby, the grass is not always greener on the other side, it might just be Astro Turf.

If you read I CORINTHIANS 12:12-27 it tells us that each one of us is valuable and that one part of the body should not feel as though they're superior, while the rest of the Body is inferior. We are all designed to work together and support each other. There is no big "I" and no little "you".

The questions we need to honestly ask ourselves are:

"Am I doing what I'm doing for the glory of God or am I trying to promote myself?"

"Have I gotten a 'big head?'"

"Do I need to humble myself?"

"Who am I really trying to impress?"

"Am I secretly in competition with someone in the Body of Christ?"

JAMES 1:22-24 (my paraphrase) tells us that anyone who listens to the Word but doesn't do what it says is like a man who looks at his face in the mirror and, after he goes away, he immediately forgets what he looks like. Could it be that we need to take a serious look at the man in our mirror?

The Bible cautions us against comparing ourselves with others to the point of becoming conceited or envious of others, because envy is like a cancer that rots our bones.

II CORINTHIANS 10:12 (TLB) *"Oh, don't worry; we wouldn't dare say that we are as wonderful as these other men who tell you how important they are! But they are only comparing themselves with each other, using themselves as the standard of measurement."*

Theodore Roosevelt said, "Comparison is the thief of joy". Making and taking time alone with God needs to be your priority. This will keep you connected with God and content on your own unique path. God is still speaking, but will you take the time to listen?

Chapter Seventeen

Will You Dare to Be Different?

We all come from different backgrounds, have different personalities, features, and styles. The Bible declares that we are fearfully and wonderfully made. I believe that we are a creation of God's vivid imagination. We were not created to be a carbon copy of anybody else. That makes us a Designer's ORIGINAL. So, be you on purpose. You will only be successful at being YOU.

I PETER 2:9 *"For you are a holy people unto the Lord your God, and the Lord has chosen you to be a peculiar people unto himself, above all the nations that are upon the earth."*

The word "peculiar" means special, unique, distinctive, extraordinary, or unusual.

DARING TO BE DIFFERENT

Consider this picture of four coins. A quarter, a dime, a nickel, and a penny. The heads of the quarter, dime, and the nickel all face to the left. Only the face of the penny faces to the right. Will you be like the penny and dare to be different? Will you choose a different way?

Do you ever feel as though you don't quite fit in with those around you in school, at work, or even in your own family? FYI: God didn't call you out for you to fit in or blend in. He called you out to **stand out**. Dare to be different for Jesus. In a world full of darkness, you are expected to be a light.

MATTHEW 5:14,16 "*You are the light of the world. A city that is set on a hill cannot be hid. Let your light so shine before men, that they may see your good works, and glorify your Father which is in heaven."*

As a child of God, we can't do everything that everyone else is doing. Anybody can follow a crowd, but it takes intestinal fortitude (guts) to dare to be different or dare to do the right thing.

JAMES 4:17 *"To him that knows to do good, and doesn't do it, to him it is sin."*

If it doesn't feel right to you, then don't do it. Sometimes you have to choose the harder right, instead of the easier wrong. Be free to be yourself and always remember that an **original** is worth more than a copy.

Here's a quote by Dr. Seuss: "Today you are you, that is truer than true. There is no one alive who is you-er than you." People will either hate that you're not like them, or they hate that they can't be like you. As long as you dress like them, act like them, talk like them, they're okay with you, but as soon as soon as you start to embrace who you are as a unique individual, then suddenly they have a serious problem with you.

Dr. Maya Angelou says, "Hate can cause a lot of problems, but it's never solved one". We are not meant to cause problems for people around us. We actually carry the solution (Jesus) to their problems.

Remember this: you're not anointed to be like somebody else, you will only be anointed to be YOU (your authentic self).

Ralph Waldo Emerson said: "To be yourself in a world that is constantly trying to make you into something else is the greatest accomplishment."

Far too many people have a "chameleon spirit". That is a person who changes their behavior or opinions according to the environment they're in or the people they're around. A chameleon has the ability to change its colors as they struggle to fit in. You keep doing what you know is right, even if you're the only one doing it. Even when the heat is on; even when your faith is under fire. Don't be afraid of being different, be afraid of being the same as everybody else.

Mehmet Murat Ildan is famous for this quote: "Be different so that people can see you clearly amongst the crowds."

One of my quotes is: "I can't be like you, and you can't be like me, because God created us differently." I'm free to be ME. It took me a while to get here, but I am finally embracing the skin that I'm in.

In the Bible, Daniel made up his mind that he would dare to be different, by refusing to defile himself with eating the king's meal (see Daniel 1:8).

Jesus said: *"If you were of the world, the world would love his own: but because you are not of the world, I have chosen you out of the world, therefore the world hates you."* (JOHN 15:19)

It feels a little risky, and sometimes uncomfortable, when you dare to be different. Noah chose to be righteous when evil was all around him (see GENESIS 6:6-8).

The three Hebrew boys separated themselves from the crowds and dared to be different by not bowing to the golden image made by King Nebuchadnezzar (see DANIEL 3:16-18). They refused to give in to peer pressure. They refused to behave in a manner that went against their beliefs and convictions.

People may not understand you, but that's okay because you are becoming the unique individual that God has created **you** to be. Whatever your calling in life may be, please walk in integrity. Do the right thing even when you don't think anyone is watching you.

Chapter Eighteen

Are You Fragile?

The definition of FRAGILE is easily broken, damaged or injured. It also means something or someone that is frail, delicate, vulnerable, and has to be handled with TLC.

A fragile person is very sensitive because they lack physical or emotional strength, and they are struggling trying to deal with everyday life issues. Often a fragile person will have low self–esteem and will tend to isolate themselves from others. Some days it's a struggle for them just to get out of bed or to see the sunshine through the window. Some people have fragile hearts because they've been deeply hurt in the past, or recently received a devastating diagnosis from their doctor, or a loved one has just passed, leaving a hole in their soul. It is my belief that everywhere you find people, you will find people with problems (in the Royal Family, in my family, even in your family; in the White House, in my house, and in your house; among entertainers, educators, athletes, politicians, clergy, blue collar workers, white collar workers, adolescents, tweens, teens, adults, seniors, the destitute, as well as the affluent). We are ALL fragile to one degree or another, because we are ALL perfectly imperfect.

Recently several celebrities have been open and transparent about their fragile mental challenges. Olympic swimmer Michael Phelps revealed how he suffered from post-Olympic depression.

Olympic gymnast Simone Biles dropped out of competition due to her **fragile** struggle with TWISTIES. Twisties are when an athlete loses their sense of where they are while their body is in mid-air. They start to worry about not being able to control their body especially when performing risky and high-level skills.

They begin to overthink it and stress themselves out.

Country music superstar Naomi Judd, as famous, beautiful, and talented as she was, dealt with years of depression and low self-esteem. She had been living in a fragile state of mind for decades. Her peers in the country music industry thought so highly of her that she was going to be inducted into the Country Music Hall of Fame, but sadly, she committed suicide the day before this monumental event was to take place. Naomi found it hard to believe that she was thought of so highly or that she was worthy.

Former First Lady Michelle Obama spoke candidly about dealing with mild depression, especially dealing with "racial issues" while in the White House.

Actor, singer, and comedian David Mann decided to be real and very transparent about his mental health issues. David portrays a very colorful and outlandish character, Mr.

Brown, on several Tyler Perry sitcoms. He has made millions of people laugh, including me. No one knew that he was secretly battling with depression for almost two years and it almost took his life! He was in a **fragile** state and was reluctant to seek professional help because of the stigma attached to mental disease, especially for black men. But thank God, he sought professional help in time.

In the year 1955, the Platters sang a song called "The Great Pretender". Here are some of the lyrics: "Oh yes, I'm the Great Pretender, pretending that I'm doing well. My need is such, I pretend too much. I'm lonely, but no one can tell". Now that is deep!

Let me remind you, that you are VALUABLE, IMPORTANT, WORTHY, and **YOU** MATTER. If you or someone you know is fragile, or suffering and struggling with depression, PLEASE don't continue to suffer in silence. Some people wear "invisible masks" to hide their true feelings and they put up an "invisible wall" to try and guard their hearts from being hurt. On the outside they may seem to have a heart of stone, but deep down within, all they really want is for somebody to love them unconditionally and understand their pain, so they can take their guard down.

Nationally, nurses, cops, teachers, and ministers are suffering from major burn-out due to the pressures of duty. Anxiety and stress can cause major depression. As a matter of fact, it's a global problem, and we need a global response. If you find yourself in a fragile state of mind, don't be too proud or ashamed to reach out for help. Help is available. Mental health is a very real issue.

Suicide and Crisis Lifeline.......988

1-800-273-TALK (8255)

FYI: It's okay to talk to Jesus and a therapist.

Chapter Nineteen

Let Your Expectations Be from God

An EXPECTATION is a strong belief that something special will happen in the near future. An expectation is something or someone you wait for with excitement and anticipation.

My friend, what are you expecting or looking forward to? Could it be a promotion, a refund check, your graduation, a birthday party, giving birth, or a marriage proposal?

In this scripture, David was professing his confidence in God when he said:

PSALM 62:5 *"My soul waits thou only upon God; for my **expectation** is from Him"* (emphasis mine). Like David, I am expecting great things to take place in MY life in the very near future.

Let's look at the scriptures found in ACTS 3:1-8 (my paraphrase): A certain man was born lame and every day he was carried and laid at the gate of the temple, where he would ask for money or food as people entered their place of worship. He saw Peter and John and asked them for money. But Peter told the lame man, *"Look on us"*. The lame man paid attention to these words and got excited, **expecting** to receive some financial assistance. However, Peter responded, *"Silver and gold have I none; but I'll give you what I do have: In the name of Jesus Christ of Nazareth rise up and walk!"*

They challenged this lame man to do what he had never done in his life. Get up and walk! Peter and John realized they had the power of the Holy Ghost operating on the inside of them, and they knew that there was miracle working power in the name of Jesus. In verse 7, we read that Peter grabbed the man by his right hand, lifted him up, and immediately his feet and ankle bones received strength. The lame man leaped up, stood, and entered the temple with them, walking, leaping and praising God! This man's expectations were surely exceeded.

Let me share this revelation that the Lord gave me about putting all your confidence in man. If we're not careful, we will believe them when they tell us they will always be there for us. Winter, spring, summer or fall, all we have to do is call, and they'll be there. But then you find out at your greatest time of need they're nowhere to be found. They've dropped you like a hot potato! However, let the record show that you're NOT where they dropped you. In other words, they thought you couldn't make it without them. They thought because they dropped you as a friend or abandoned you while you were in the valley of discouragement, that you were a done deal, but God brought you up, out, over and through.

You can tell those fake and phony friends, "I'm NOT where you left me!" Jesus stepped in when I needed Him most. Now I KNOW without a doubt that my expectation is from the Lord and not from man. I honestly believe that God wants us to RAISE our levels of expectations and not just settle or put limits on Him. I'm basing this belief on:

EPHESIANS 3:28 *"Now unto Him that is able to do exceeding abundantly above all that we ask or think, according to the power that worketh in us."*

My friend, do you have that power working in you? Are you powerful or pitiful? Let your expectations be from God.

I CORINTHIANS 2:9 *"But as it is written: Eye has not seen, nor ear heard, nor has it entered into the heart of man, the things which God has prepared for them that love Him."*

I don't know about you Dear Reader, but I'm believing God for epic blessings in 2023 and beyond! EPIC means above and beyond, spectacular; blessings so awesome it will literally blow your mind, and you will remember it for years to come.

PSALM 68:19 *"Blessed be the Lord who daily loads us with benefits, even the God of our salvation."* Benefits include God's healing, favor, love, presence, protection, guidance, restoration, and prosperity.

When our **expectation** is from God, we will believe that He is going to open doors for us that no man can close. We will trust that God is going to make a way where there seems to be no way. We rest assured that God will prepare a table for us in the presence of our enemies. We know that God can make our latter days greater than our former days. God will make us a lender and not a borrower. God can surely be counted on to rebuke the devourer for our sake. We believe God will bless us so we can bless others.

So, I challenge you to raise your level of expectation from God, because with God

NOTHING SHALL BE IMPOSSIBLE!

Chapter Twenty

Restoration Can Still Take Place in You

RESTORATION is the act of returning something to its former or original condition or state. It's the process of making something better, whole, or new again.

JEREMIAH 30:17 *"For I will restore health unto you, and I will heal you of your wounds, said the Lord; because they called you an outcast, saying, this is Zion, the place nobody wants."*

JOB 42:10 *"And the Lord turned the captivity of Job, when he prayed for his friends: also the Lord gave Job twice as much as he had before."*

Let's look at the parable of the prodigal son (see LUKE 15:11-32). First, a parable is an earthly story with a heavenly meaning. When the younger son in this story received his inheritance, his father was still alive. This young man left home and lost all his fortune due to his uncontrollable and excessive spending. He ended up broke, busted, and disgusted. He finally came to himself, realized the error of his foolish ways, swallowed his pride, and decided to go back home. From a distance his father recognized his son. He could have refused to let him come back home, to teach him with "tough love", but he didn't! His heart was full of compassion as he welcomed his son back home, lovingly and unconditionally. He chose to look beyond his son's faults and shortcomings and see his need for **restoration.** That's the same way our Heavenly Father cares for us.

PSALM 23:3 *"He restores my soul."*

In other words, the Lord gives us a refreshing. Many times, He gets us out of the mess we got ourselves into. In our weakest state, He gives us strength. He loves on us. He heals us everywhere that we're hurting and broken.

In the first chapter of Ruth, she was a widow because her husband died, but by the fourth chapter she found love again and married Boaz, a wealthy landowner.

Sometimes, we think that after the death of our loved one, that we will never find love again, that we will never be happy again. I say, "Never say never, because **restoration** can still take place." Even after a divorce, it doesn't mean your life is over. Sometimes the very thing that we lose could be a blessing in disguise because it is hindering our progress and our Mighty God has something or someone better in store for you. God doesn't want you to continue to "settle" or live beneath your privilege. God has a blessing with your name on it! He wants to **restore** your **joy**.

PSALM 51:12 *"Restore unto me the joy of thy salvation."*

In other words, Lord, make me as happy as you did when you first saved me.

Lord, I believe you will give me PEACE for all my PIECES.

Lord, I believe you are able to increase my peace and multiply my days.

Lord, I believe you will give me a peace that passes my understanding.

Lord, I believe you will give me joy, unspeakable joy, and full of glory. That's the kind of joy that runs over and overflows. It is a joy from God that cannot be described.

RESTORATION CAN STILL TAKE PLACE IN YOU

Even if your body is tired, your mind is overwhelmed, and you don't feel the fire deep down on the inside like you used to, restoration can still take place. Even if you don't feel the passion when you preach or the anointing when you sing, restoration is possible. Even if it seems like you've lost your press, praise, and your fervent prayers, God has restoration in store for you. Even though it may seem as though your spiritual storage is empty and you're just going through the motions, let me assure you that there is hope. You just need a spiritual overhaul and you need it now!

MATTEW 11:28-30 *"Come unto Me, all ye that labor and are heavy laden, and I will give you rest. Take my yoke upon you and learn of me; for I am meek and lowly in heart: and you shall find rest unto your souls. For my yoke is easy, and my burden is light."*

In other words, if you are burdened down then you haven't released your burdens to the Burden-Bearer. The Burden-Bearer is the One who makes restoration possible.

Read PSALM 24:7-10 where it says, *"Lift up your heads"* (vs. 7 and 9). This is not a request, it's a command. This is "real talk". When we lift our heads, we must be confident that the King of Glory is coming into our situation with power, healing, breakthroughs, victory, and most of all, He's coming in with

RESTORATION.

I don't care how far you may have strayed, or how low you may have sunk, restoration can still take place in you. God said it, but do you believe it?

Chapter Twenty-one

Trust The Process and Wait on God's Timing

Sometimes we hear in our hearts or through others that God has called us, and that may very well be true; but it may not be your time to go forth right now.

HABAKKUK 2:3 *"For the vision is yet for an appointed time, but at the end it shall speak and not lie: though it tarry, wait for it; because it will surely come, it will not tarry."*

When the time is right, it will happen. So "chill out". Don't try to make things happen prematurely or rush the process. Be patient and wait for your proper timing. You must be willing to trust the process and wait on God's perfect timing.

A PROCESS is a series of actions or steps to achieve a desired goal.

We are much too impatient. We don't want to wait. We want instant everything. Instant coffee, instant oatmeal, instant popcorn, instant success, instant anointing, instant gratification, even instant breakthroughs.

Here is an example of trusting the process: your flight may be scheduled to depart at 2:00pm, but there are people working behind the scenes to make sure that everything is in proper working order to ensure you have a safe flight. Even the pilot of the plane must wait for instructions from the Air Traffic Controller. They talk to the pilot on the ground and in the air. God wants to do the same with us. We must listen for His voice, obey His commands, follow His instructions and wait on His timing.

Now, I know some of you may be enthusiastic, have a zeal for the Lord, have a fire shut up in your bones, feel as though you're ready to leap over walls and jump through troops. Perhaps a prophet told you last week in a revival that God has called you to preach. Now you rush to your local office supply store and get you some cards made, saying you are a national evangelist. Sweetheart, you are not ready. You're still a novice. You still need to be **taught.** You still have some growing to do. You need to sit under a mature and anointed man or woman of God who can pour into you and teach you about protocol, and how to handle the anointing. You should be sure that you're saved and you need to honor the process.

Here's another example of trusting the process: David was the youngest of Jesse's eight sons. When it was time to choose the next King of Israel, David was the last son to be considered. However, God had divine plans for David's life, even while he was still tending the smelly sheep in the fields. Even though Samuel ended up anointing David as the next King of Israel, he had to go through a process before he could handle the requirements of being a King and a man after God's own heart. It was almost **fifteen years** between the time that David was anointed King and when he actually became King!

David had to face the giant Goliath, and you are going to face some giants in your life as well. Your giants may be physical, emotional, financial, or even spiritual. David was also banished (sent away as an official punishment) by King Saul. Saul hated David because God's Spirit was upon him so greatly. Don't get it twisted: sometimes people will hate you because of the way that God uses you, favors you, blesses you, or anoints you. However, they don't know the **process** that you had to go through to be able to walk in your anointing. David hid in the desert and lived like a fugitive on the run and had to fight many battles. His success didn't happen overnight. It was a process. But David **trusted the process** and **waited** on God's divine timing.

Abraham and Sarah had to wait on God and trust the process for their lives also. Abraham was 75 years old and childless when he left his hometown as directed by God. Abraham was 100 years old when his son Isaac was born. He had to wait 25 years for God's promise to be fulfilled! (Read GENESIS 12:4 and 21:5).

GENESIS 17:17 *"Abraham fell upon his face and laughed and said in his heart, shall a child be born unto me that's 100 years old, and shall Sarah who is 90 years old bear a child?"*

Have you ever been in a state of shock and disbelief when you were told that God was going to do something phenomenal or miraculous in your life? Did you have a hard time believing it because of your age, past, physical condition, level of education, or your family history? Dear Reader, *is anything too hard for the Lord?*

When God first made the promise to Abraham and Sarah, in the natural, it seemed like an impossible situation. But they needed to release their NOW FAITH (see Hebrews 11:1).

Simply said, FAITH is believing, when everything around you is saying the complete opposite. Faith is the ability not to panic. Faith is your positive response to what God has already said. We wait on God's perfect timing because it strengthens our faith, as we have no other choice but to wait and trust God. That way God, and God alone, gets the praise, glory, and the honor for pulling us through.

Dr. Martin Luther King says, "Take the first step in faith. You don't have to see the whole staircase, just take the first step." If God promised it, He'll perform it. If God spoke it, He'll do it. If God said it, He'll bring it to pass.

PSALM 27:14 (emphasis mine) "***Wait*** *on the Lord: be of good courage, and He shall strengthen your heart:* ***Wait****, I say, on the Lord.*"

ISAIAH 40:31 *"But they that wait upon the Lord shall renew their strength; they shall mount up with wings as eagles; they shall run, and not be weary; and they shall walk and not faint."*

ADVANTAGES OF WAITING ON GOD'S TIMING:

- It protects us from danger.
- It helps to build our character.
- It helps us to grow and mature.
- It teaches us more about the character and attributes of God.
- It allows God to show us who we really are and what we are capable of.

While we are waiting on our process to come to fruition, it can be easy to grow weary and become discouraged but remember it takes work and patience during the planting and growing season, before you can reap a harvest.

GALATIANS 6:9 *"Let us not become weary in well doing, for at the proper time, we will reap a harvest if we do not give up."*

CONTINUE TO TRUST YOUR PROCESS

I bake a lot of pound cakes and, trust me, that involves a PROCESS also. Before my loved ones can enjoy a slice of cake, here's the process that I go through:

- Gather all the ingredients.
- Measure them.
- Mix them in the bowl.
- Preheat my oven to 325 degrees for ten minutes.
- Spray my pan with Baker's Joy.
- Pour the batter into the pan.
- Bake in the oven for one hour and twenty minutes.
- I make sure nobody jumps or walks hard in the kitchen because this can cause the cake to fall (and then that somebody will be in trouble with me, LOL).
- I stick a fork in the center of the cake and make sure it comes out clean, then I

know it's ready to come out of the oven.

- I cool the cake for 15-20 minutes.
- I flip it onto my cake plate.
- I prepare the glaze or icing if desired.

Keep in mind that you don't get pregnant in May and give birth to an 8-pound baby in June.

IT'S A PROCESS

Are you willing to trust **your process**, no matter how long it takes? Just because your blessing is delayed doesn't mean your blessing has been denied. Stop tripping and pull yourself together. The Master of the Universe is behind the scenes working on your masterpiece. God is not through with you yet. He's still working on you. He's still PREPARING you. He's still moving on your behalf; so, stop trying to make things happen in your own strength. Stop trying to "help" God out. Stop trying to "fix" other people. Only God can do that. Even when it doesn't look or feel like it, God's plans for your life are bigger and greater than anything that you can imagine. Move over and let God be the pilot and the orchestrator of your life and enjoy the process.

Chapter Twenty-two

Check Your Perception

PERCEPTION is the ability to see, hear, or become aware of something through the senses. It's a mental impression. Perception not only creates our experience of the world around us; it allows us to act within our environment. The way we view the world and everything around us has a direct effect on our thoughts, actions, and behavior.

What's your perception of YOURSELF?

In the Old Testament book of NUMBERS 13:33, we read: *"And there we saw the giants, the sons of Anak, which come of the giants; and we were in our own sight as grasshoppers, and so we were in their sight."*

The Lord told Moses to send men to spy out the land of Canaan. When the men returned, they verified that the land was very fruitful, but they **focused** on the size of the giants living in the land. Even though Caleb (one of the twelve courageous spies) told the people that they were able to overcome the city and possess it, their **perception** wouldn't allow them to believe Caleb. Why? Because in their **own eyes** they saw themselves as inferior. Again, I ask you: what's your perception of yourself? Say to yourself, "The me I see, is the me I'll be." Pray this simple prayer: "Lord, open my eyes and help me believe I am what YOU see."

In the 6th chapter of JUDGES (found in the Old Testament), the angel of the Lord appeared to Gideon and said, *"The Lord is with you mighty warrior."*

God was reassuring Gideon that he would be used to save Israel from the hand of the Midianites. Gideon's response was, *"Lord, how can I save Israel, my family is poor in Manasseh, and I am least in my father's house."* In other words, Gideon was saying he was so poor, that he couldn't even pay attention, LOL.

Precious Reader, have you ever felt that you were unqualified or you just didn't meet the necessary criteria? Praise God that His **perception** of us is so much greater than ours! God already considered Gideon a warrior, while he was full of doubt. God saw the potential in him. God calls us what we SHALL BE, while we're busy focusing on what we currently ARE, or what we used to be.

David went up against the giant Goliath. He wasn't intimidated by his size, height, or his previous victories over other opponents. David's **perception** of himself was that he was more than a conqueror! David was confident in the God he served. Are you?

When my husband was stationed in Germany, I attended a church where the pastor was German-American (Pastor Martin Levy), and he introduced us to a song by a woman named Evie Karlson. Some of her lyrics were: "I'm only 4 foot 11, but I'm going to Heaven, and that makes me feel 10 feet tall." She had an awesome perception of herself, knowing that her height had nothing to do with her relationship with the Lord.

I was amazed when my 4-year-old great niece Brielle told me that she knew what the word perception meant. She says it means, "You're getting it wrong. The way you see it isn't the way I see it!"

In the first chapter of I SAMUEL, it tells us that a woman named Hannah was barren and unable to conceive children. In Old Testament times, a childless woman was considered a failure. Her inability to have children was a social embarrassment for her husband. By law, her husband Elkanah could have left her because a husband was allowed to divorce a barren wife; but he remained lovingly devoted to Hannah. Has there ever been a time in your life that you have felt barren (unable to give birth to your dream or vision)?

Have you ever felt like others around you were constantly being blessed yet it seemed like you were being punished, cursed, or overlooked?

Peninnah (Elkanah's other wife) was very fertile. She constantly picked at Hannah because she was not able to have children. I personally believe that Peninnah can also represent a person who really knows how to push your buttons, rub you the wrong way, tick you off, get under your skin, provoke you, raise your blood pressure, and cause you to act out of character. I already know that some of you "super saints" will never admit to reacting to the spirit of Peninnah. But for the rest of us… The real issue between these two women was that Peninnah was able to do what Hannah could not. Don't miss this: the devil assigns people who will try and make you feel inferior or unworthy.

Former First Lady Eleanor Roosevelt said these profound words: "No one can make you feel inferior without your consent." Now take a minute and marinate on that.

Deep down in her heart, I believe that Peninnah was jealous of Hannah because she had something that Peninnah did not: a "worthy portion" or a double portion from "their" husband (see I SAMUEL 1:5). In other words, it was her **perception** that Elkanah really loved Hannah more. Peninnah may have thought, "I don't see my husband's eyes light up when I walk into a room anymore. I'm having all his babies; if it weren't for Hannah, my life would be perfect. She makes me sick!" Yes, Peninnah was jealous of Hannah. Hannah knew that her husband loved her, but even his love couldn't seem to comfort or fill the void in her life because she was broken and felt less than a woman. If Hannah were in our day and time, she might say, "Lord, I'm not asking for much. I'm not asking to hit the power ball. I'm not asking for a body like Beyonce or for a million-dollar home, all I want is a child." Finally, Hannah received her son from the Lord.

Beloved, do you realize that there may be some people you know that seem to have it all: the six-figure income, multiple cars and degrees, and are able to afford the finer things in life. But you never knew that they were jealous of you, because of the one gift you possess. You never knew they were secretly hating on you.

So many people are having cosmetic surgeries such as face lifts, tummy tucks, breast enhancements and Brazilian butt lifts, so others will perceive them differently. Every woman is not meant to be a size four. So, free yourself, and stop worrying about how people perceive you, just be sure you have the correct perception about yourself. Make sure you don't start seeing or perceiving yourself through the eyes of those who can't see your true value. You must know your worth, even if others don't have a clue. Remember that

"YOU ARE WHO GOD SAYS YOU ARE, regardless of who you're around."

Chapter Twenty-three

How Did I End Up in a Stagnant State of Mind?

When a person is STAGNANT, they have isolated themselves from God and have stopped responding to the needs of others. They're not doing anything to enhance their spirit. It's like a knot just sitting on a log or like sitting and waiting for paint to dry. There doesn't seem to be anything that excites you enough to take action to get you out of this predicament. Your spirit has become dull and sluggish. You have found yourself "stuck in a rut". When you're stuck, you can't go forward or backward.

Regardless of our titles or positions, there will be seasons in our lives when we will feel uninspired and unmotivated because we are human.

Here are some ways to tell if you're in a **stagnant** state of mind:

- You are constantly procrastinating on your goals.
- You don't ever feel motivated to do anything.
- You know you should be doing something, but you constantly avoid doing it.
- You feel deep down on the inside that you're living beneath your privilege, but still can't seem to do anything about it.

When we face **stagnation**, these pointers can be helpful: find what inspires you. If there isn't anything that excites you to take action or set goals, you will continue to face boredom and remain stagnant. Give yourself a break. You may need an emotional time-out. You may need to get refreshed, recharged, and re-focused. You might need to change your routine. Being in the same environment, doing the same things over and over, day in and day out, hanging with the same people, can cause you to become stagnant; especially if the people you spend most of your time with are stagnant themselves. When you change things around you, it can help to stir/motivate you to do something different.

Spoiler Alert: People who are stagnant, slothful, stuck in their comfort zones, or content with last week's manna or Word will NOT receive fresh revelation or a visitation from the Lord. It's very true that a negative mind will never produce positive results.

In JOHN 5:1-9, it tells us how an angel came down at a certain season into the pool and "troubled" (stirred) the water. Whoever stepped into the water first, after the stirring of it, was made WHOLE of whatever disease he had. Sometimes we have **dis-ease** in our spirits, minds, and our bodies. Maybe we need to ask the Lord to stir the waters of our hearts, so we won't have dis-ease and become stagnant. The man in these scriptures had an infirmity or physical weakness for **38 years! That's 456 months, and 13,870 days.** What an awful long time to be stagnant, dysfunctional, weak, feeble, lame, and helpless.

When you finally decide to break out of your usual monotonous stagnation and make an earnest attempt to try something new and different, you will be able to embrace brand new possibilities and gain a fresh new perspective.

Chapter Twenty-four

Do You Respect Protocol?

PROTOCOL in church is a set of rules regarding church worship services and the acceptable behavior in the house of the Lord. The Church is the most important place where dignity, respect and reverence should be maintained. It is a place to give honor to those whom honor is due. Protocol is a system of rules that explain correct conduct that is to be followed. Where there is no order, there will be disorder, and our God is a God of order. His Word says in I CORINTHIANS 14:40: *"Let **all** things be done **decently** and in **order**"* (emphasis mine).

I CORINTHIANS 14:33: *"For God is not the author of confusion, but of peace, as in all churches of the saints."*

I personally believe that too many preachers are receiving their minister's licenses without going through the proper training. They need to be taught "pulpit etiquette" and how to conduct themselves during a worship service. For instance, if you ask them to read a scripture and they get up and sing a mini concert, then try and preach a "sermonette", that's OUT OF ORDER. That's NOT respecting protocol. That's a person whose **flesh** wants to be noticed!

The fruit of the Spirit includes **self-control,** but the fruit of the flesh is **no control.** Whenever you go into another pastor's pulpit, the courteous thing for you to do is to acknowledge them as being the Pastor or "angel" of the local house. If you were ever in a leadership position, I'm certain you would want to be respected as well. After all, if you are an invited guest, you should always respect protocol.

I know preachers who think because they

have a cross and a clergy collar on, they can march right up to the pulpit, even in a church they've never been in before. Why? Because their flesh wants to be noticed. As preachers, we need to be sure that we're not like the Pharisees in Luke 11:43: *"Woe unto you Pharisees! For you love the chief* seats (best seats, seats of honor) *in the synagogues and the salutations in the marketplaces"*. The Pharisees were seen as self-righteous and hypocritical because they were more concerned with "outer" appearances than with the condition of their own hearts.

If the Pastor of that church doesn't invite you to the pulpit, then maintain your decorum and sit out in the congregation, without getting offended. There are times when I personally prefer to sit out in the congregation of another church. It's not necessary for anybody to know my name or my title or position. I am just as much a preacher sitting out in the tenth row of the congregation, as I am sitting up in the pulpit. Sometimes I just want to sit amid a spirit-filled church and be fed with Bread from Heaven.

When we, as ministers, stand before the people, we also need to be careful of how we dress. Our attire is also part of protocol. Women: The Bible says we are to dress in modest apparel (see I TIMOTHY 2:9). That doesn't mean our skirts or dresses must be touching our ankles when speaking in the pulpit. Our clothing can be fashionable without being suggestive or provocative. We don't want to wear outfits that are too revealing and attract unnecessary attention to ourselves. After all, your flesh should NOT be on parade. Your dress or skirt should not be so tight or short that it looks like you are going to bust out of it if you cough. You should not show half your thighs or have too much cleavage showing. Oh, I know the world says: "If you've got it, then flaunt it", but that should **not** be the case in the house of God. If YOU'RE doing it, then sweetie, that's a **fleshy** spirit.

As far as pulpit attire, I don't want to omit the male ministers. If you have too much "junk in your trunk", then you need to avoid skinny pants. Everything that looks good on a smaller man may not do your particular body size any justice. So please wear an outfit that will compliment *your* body type. After all, we don't want the wrong emphasis placed on the messenger, instead of the message. We don't want to be the wrong type of distraction in the pulpit. Rule of thumb: Dress in a way as if Jesus were sitting beside or in front of you. Would He be happy with how you're representing Him? Again, I say as the Word says: *"Let **all** things be done decently and in order."*

Remember to always RESPECT PROTOCOL!

Chapter Twenty-five

It's Important to Stay in Your Lane!

There are so many DIVERSITIES of gifts and callings which are useful, and all of them may not be found in the Bible. Some examples include:

Hair Stylists - Barbers - Chefs - Event Planners - Photographers - Doctors - Dentists - Graphic Artists - Designers - Mechanics - Singers - Musicians - Personal Trainers - Contractors - Authors - Poets - Social Media Influencers - CPA'S - Funeral Directors - Wedding Planners - Realtors – Investors - Intercessors - Prayer Warriors - Exhorters - Athletes - Teachers - Lawn Care Professionals - Police Officers - Meteorologists - Ushers - Entertainers - Health Care Workers…

And the list could go on and on. But the

point that I'm trying to make is this: IT'S IMPORTANT TO STAY IN YOUR OWN LANE!

Do what YOU'VE been called to do!

God has a specific plan and purpose for each of us. He anoints, empowers, and enables each of us in unique ways. It's important for each of us to accept and embrace what God has assigned us to do. Don't beat up on yourself if you aren't called to do what somebody else is able or anointed to do.

I CORINTHIANS 12:12: *"For as the body is one and has many members, and all the members of that one body, being many, are one body; so also is Christ."* Verse 14 says: *"For the body is not one member, but many."* Verses 15-25 tell us that ALL members of the body are USEFUL.

Spiritual Gifts are for the Body of Christ. Ministry Gifts are **people.**

EPHESIANS 4:11 *"And He gave some, apostles;*

and some, prophets; and some, evangelists; and some, pastors and teachers."

Do you know why these gifts were given? They were given for three reasons: For the work of the ministry, for the perfecting of the saints, and for the edifying of the body of Christ.

Observe this picture of the HAND:

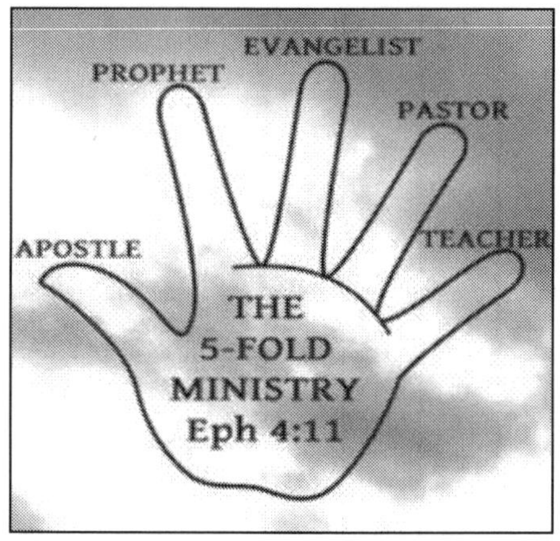

- The THUMB is the APOSTLE.
- The INDEX FINGER is the PROPHET.
- The MIDDLE FINGER is the EVANGELIST.
- The RING FINGER is the PASTOR.
- The PINKY FINGER is the TEACHER.

APOSTLE: means a SENT ONE; one sent forth; a church planter. Apostles go into new territory and start new churches. Apostles perform signs, wonders, and miracles. To stand in this office, a person must have a deep personal encounter with the Lord and an ongoing spiritually strong relationship with God and His Word. They must be able to provide spiritual leadership.

Just because this office is listed first in Ephesians 4:11, does not mean it is the most important Ministry Gift, or that Apostles are to dominate or lord over the other ministry gifts (which are people), in the Body of Christ. The Apostle inspires and leads the way by establishing new works for the Lord. There is also such a thing as "flowing" in an apostolic anointing.

There are also false apostles who have their own selfish agendas and are not concerned about serving the needs of God's people. Thank God for true Apostles who travel and build up Pastors who have grown battle-weary and discouraged due to the pressures of leadership.

PROPHET: SEES and KNOWS things supernaturally and is given revelations by God. A Prophet sets the house in order. This is a Ministry Gift that is chosen by God for the Body of Christ. A real Prophet does more than prophesy about new cars, jobs, and houses to people. A Prophet also warns people of impending danger, and often will rebuke and intercede on behalf of others before God. It may take years for a Prophet to fully develop their prophetic gifts.

If you are truly called into the Prophetic office, let God set you in it. If you're faithful, and God sees He can trust you with this gift, then He will set you in it. Why? Because if a rookie or a novice is put into this office prematurely by man, and that person is not equipped, then Satan can tempt them to become puffed up, and they will try to set themselves into this office and make the Prophetic pathetic. Many people think that a Prophet knows everything about everybody. NOT SO. The Lord only tells a Prophet what HE wants them to know. Only God is omniscient. He knows everything about everybody, including the Prophet. Sadly, there are false Prophets who are in this office, just to make a profit. Let the record show that a Prophet and a psychic are not the same. The Bible has harsh warnings about false Prophets.

MATTHEW 7:15 *"Beware of false prophets, which come to you in sheep's clothing, but inwardly they are ravening wolves."*

I JOHN 4:1 *"Beloved, believe not every spirit, but try the spirits whether they are of God: because many false Prophets are gone out into the world."*

MATTHEW 24:11 *"And many false Prophets shall rise and shall deceive many."*

Regardless of gender, God can use a

person to prophesy, but just because you can prophesy, that alone does not make you a prophet.

God releases His prophetic voice to and through His true Prophets. God reveals His will and declares things or events supernaturally through His anointed and chosen man or woman of God. Prophets receive their messages from God in visions and dreams. God also uses them to foretell the future and reveal secret events. God uses Prophets to convict people of their sins and call them to repentance. Self-seeking Prophets can make a lie sound like the truth. They are inclined to tell people what they **want** to hear, rather than what they **need** to hear. Their flattering words don't challenge people to change their evil ways, and their hearts are not right with God. They have a counterfeit anointing and will deceive many people.

MATTHEW 24:24 *"There shall arise false prophets who will show great signs and wonders to deceive the very elect if it were possible".*

JEREMIAH 23:21 *"I have not sent these prophets, yet they ran: I have not spoken to them, yet they prophesied."*

They were perverting prophetic gifts. These false prophets have become more like entertainers and performers than true prophets.

EVANGELIST: travels from one place to another, preaching the Word of God. They are SOUL WINNERS. They conduct revivals and crusades. Evangelists have a burning desire to see people saved, delivered, loosed, and set free. Their desire is to reach the lost at any cost. Their main theme is SALVATION. Their primary focus is Jesus.

Evangelists need to be Holy Ghost-filled as they bring conviction to sinners and encouragement to believers. Their heart's desire is that the Gospel of Jesus Christ reach as many people as possible.

II TIMOTHY 4:5b *"Do the work of an evangelist, make full proof of thy ministry."*

PASTORS: are the ring finger on the hand illustration because they are married to the flock. They SHEPHERD over a local church. Pastors exercise authority over the local church by **feeding, leading, loving, and correcting** the sheep that God has entrusted in their care. Pastors are necessary for maturing and equipping the people of God. This is one of the most important offices in the five-fold ministry gifts. Without the ministry of Pastors, all other ministries would practically be in vain. The reason I support this claim is because no matter how prophetic the Prophet is, or how many churches the Apostles establish, or how many people get saved through the Evangelists, if there is no one to shepherd the sheep, they will fall by the wayside. The Pastor is the head. He or she is your covering and your spiritual "umbrella".

HEBREWS 13:17 *"Obey them that have the rule*

over you and submit yourselves: for they watch for your souls, as they that must give account, that they may do it with joy, and not with grief: for that is unprofitable for you."

JEREMIAH 3:15 *"And I will give you Pastors after my own heart, which shall feed you with knowledge and understanding."*

If you are a part of a local church, you should follow your Leader/Pastor, as long as your Pastor is following God and doing their best to lead by example.

I PETER 5:2-3 *"Feed the flock of God that is under your care, watching over them, not because you must, but because you are willing, as God wants you to be; not pursuing dishonest gain, but eager to serve God; not lording it over those entrusted to you, but being examples to the flock."*

I believe that too many Leaders/Pastors are in this position of authority strictly for the money. They have private jets, live in million-dollar mansions, and are constantly insisting that their members give more money, even when some of them are living below poverty levels. It's sad, but there are leaders who accumulate a lot of money by swindling, manipulating, and defrauding their members. Please, don't you be one of them!

TEACHERS: are the pinky finger in the above Hand illustration. They help bring balance to the Body of Christ. Preachers proclaim the Word. Teachers EXPLAIN the Word. Before a teacher can teach, they must first be taught. Jesus had a three-fold ministry: preaching, teaching, and healing. He taught his disciples for three years before sending them forth to reach others. He realized before they could "effectively" carry out the Great Commission in Matthew 28:19-20, it was necessary for them to receive sound doctrine (teaching). The work of the Teacher is to build up, not tear down the Body of Christ.

A wise teacher knows that everyone in the class won't learn as quickly as others. While some students may be on "strong meat", others may still be on milk. Teachers will motivate you to get into the Word of God and get the Word of God into YOU.

Here are three practical guidelines for Teachers to follow:

- Present your material in an interesting fashion.
- Make sure your lessons have practical application. You don't want to overload your students with a lot of facts, because if they can't apply them to their everyday lives, your lesson is "fruitless" or in vain.
- Thirdly, you want to teach with humility, simplicity, and compassion. Don't allow your knowledge to puff you up with pride and cause you to look down on others.

A godly teacher must be able to rightly divide the Word of God and apply it to their **own** life.

My Mother was an educator and would often say that a great teacher is one who will admit they don't know it all, and can learn from their students, as well as from "life lessons". This is a very profound quote by Kirill Korshikov: "Never stop learning because life never stops teaching."

You will never see an 18-month-old baby driving an 18-wheeler truck! Why? Because it would be too dangerous. They're babies. They're not mature enough. They haven't been trained. It's sad, but there are many who are teaching others, that need to be taught themselves. They're trying to act "deep" when they don't even have the basic knowledge necessary to teach effectively. You can't teach what you don't know.

As you can see, it really is important to STAY IN YOUR LANE.

Chapter Twenty-six

Positive Affirmations

POSITIVE AFFIRMATIONS are statements that challenge us to change our negative thinking patterns. The Bible even instructs us to do this.

PROVERBS 18:21 *"Life and death are in the power of the tongue."*

So, open your mouth and speak positive words over yourself such as:

"When God created ME, He deposited everything in me that was necessary for me to fulfill what He has called ME to do."

"As long as I have a pulse, I have a purpose."

"I have purpose, power, potential and endless possibilities within me."

"I have special and unique gifts to offer to

this world."

"When God gets ready to bless me, the approval or opinion of others is not required."

"I have God's power, provision, and protection working on my behalf."

"My history does not determine my destiny."

"My condition is not my conclusion."

"I am capable of doing amazing things."

"I am one of a kind. I'm an original and I'll never be duplicated."

"My obstacles can turn out to be my greatest opportunities."

"My talent is God's gift to me, what I do with it, is my gift to God."

"I am who God says I am, regardless of who I'm around."

"I must begin to detach myself from people who will interfere with my purpose."

According to PSALM 138:8, ***"The Lord will perfect those things that concern me."***

"By the grace of God, I am what I am." **(I CORINTHIANS 15:10)**

"I am God's masterpiece."

"I can do all things through Christ which strengthens me." **(PHILLIPIANS 4:13)**

"I will praise you; for I am fearfully and wonderfully made." **(PSALM 139:14a)**

"I'm embracing the ME that I'm becoming."

"I'm beautifully flawed and perfectly imperfect."

"I will use my gifts to glorify God and to benefit others."

In the words of Dr. Martin Luther King, Jr., "If I cannot do great things, I can do small

things in a great way."

About The Author

Nancy F. Lowery is a bold and sold-out soldier in the Army of the Lord. She and her husband Malcom of 45 years, whom she affectionately calls her Honey Bunny, have one daughter, Professor Teyshana Lowery. They have all served their country and are proud veterans.

Nancy has been preaching the uncompromising Gospel of Jesus Christ for over 36 years. She is an ordained Elder and Apostle. Nancy is unashamedly saved, sanctified, and Holy Ghost-filled!

This author realizes that she never would have made it through this journey called life, without the prayers, love, support, and constructive criticism of her family, mentors, prayer warriors and genuine friends. Nancy is a Spiritual Mother and mentor to many.

Apostle Lowery is truly appreciative of all the people who believed in her and spoke prophetic words over her life and poured into her spirit with their wisdom and anointing. Most of all, she's grateful to her loved ones for giving her that extra "push" to persevere in completing this fifth inspirational book,

Ultimately, GOD gets ALL the glory, praise, honor, and the credit for ALL the amazing and epic things that He has done and continues to do in her life.

Made in the USA
Columbia, SC
25 June 2025

59771283R00100